The Lakes

published by
pocket mountains ltd
6 Church Wynd, Bo'ness EH51 0AN
pocketmountains.com

ISBN 13: 9-780954-421762

A catalogue record for this book is available from the British Library

Printed in Poland

Introduction

This guide features forty circular fell routes in the Lake District of England.

Routes have been chosen for a number of reasons, including variety of terrain, great views, historical interest, minimal road walking and the feasibility of a circular route.

Environmental factors have been considered in the design of routes, including the ability to begin in towns and villages, reach the start by bus or for access points to support additional car parking. Routes in this book tend either to follow paths that have been repaired or traverse less popular terrain, where fewer footsteps give the land a chance to regenerate. All of the routes are circular, which reduces pressure and makes for a more varied walk. This explains the omission of a few circuits, fells or ridges that are regarded as classics. Walkers are also encouraged to take variations from the walks described, where terrain, access rights and experience allow.

The Lake District Tourism and Conservation Partnership can provide information on conservation and erosion, supporting projects such as footpath restoration and habitat protection through funding raised by the Cumbria tourist trade. Spending with businesses that display the 'handshake' logo will, in many cases, result in a direct contribution to the work of the Partnership (www.lakespartnership.org.uk).

Walkers can minimise their impact on the environment by using purpose-built paths wherever possible and walking in single file to help prevent widening scars. Trekking poles are known to cause erosion: walkers who choose to use them for health reasons should do so responsibly, removing the baskets and using rubber tips. Sensible parking, using stiles and gates where they exist (and never crossing tensed wire fences), avoiding fires and litter, and keeping dogs on a close lead, particularly on grazing land and during lambing, all help to preserve the land and good relations with its inhabitants. The Countryside Code encourages respect, protection and enjoyment of the land and should be followed at all times.

How to use this guide

The routes in this book are divided into five regions. These divisions largely represent points of access into the mountains, rather than using the natural geographical boundaries of valleys and massifs. The opening section for each of the five regions introduces the area with brief route outlines. It is supplemented by a road map, locating the walks.

Each route begins with an introduction identifying the names and heights of significant tops, the relevant Ordnance Survey (OS) map, total distance and average time.

A sketch map shows the main topographical details of the area and the route. The map is intended only to give the reader an idea of the terrain, and should not be followed for navigation.

3

Every route has an estimated round-trip time: this is for rough guidance only and should help in planning, especially when daylight hours are limited. In winter or after heavy rain, extra time should also be added for difficulties underfoot.

Risks and how to avoid them

Many of the fells in this guide are remote and craggy, and the weather can change suddenly, reducing visibility to several yards. Winter walking brings particular challenges, including limited daylight, white-outs, cornices and avalanches. Almost every year, there are fatalities in the Lake District, and dozens of walkers and climbers are rescued after falls and slips. Equally, though, Mountain Rescue teams are often called out to walkers who are exhausted, lost or simply late to return.

Preparation for a walk should begin well before you set out, and your choice of route should reflect your fitness, the conditions underfoot and the regional weather forecasts.

None of the walks in this guide should be attempted without the relevant OS Map or equivalent at 1:25,000 (or 1:50,000) and a compass.

Even in summer, warm, waterproof clothing is advisable and footwear that is comfortable and supportive with good grips a must. Don't underestimate how much food and water you need and remember to take any medication required, including reserves in case of illness or delay. A whistle, watch and torch are essential, and in winter conditions an ice axe, crampons

and a survival bag should also be taken.

It is a good idea to leave a route description with a friend or relative in case a genuine emergency arises: you should not rely on a mobile phone to get you out of difficulty. If walking as part of a group, make sure your companions are aware of any medical conditions and how to deal with problems that may occur.

There is a route for most levels of fitness in this guide, but it is important to know your limitations. Even for an experienced walker, colds, aches and pains can turn an easy walk into an ordeal.

These routes assume some knowledge of navigation in the fells with use of map and compass, though these skills are not difficult to learn. Use of Global Positioning System (GPS) devices is becoming more common but, while GPS can help pinpoint your location on the map in zero visibility, it cannot tell you where to go next.

Techniques such as scrambling or climbing on rock, snow and ice are required on a number of the routes in this guide. Such skills will improve confidence and the ease with which any route can be completed. They will also help you to avoid or escape potentially dangerous areas if you lose your way. The British Mountaineering Council provides information and advice.

For most of these routes, proficiency in walking and navigation is sufficient.

Access

The legal 'right to roam', locally applied from May 2005 under the Countryside and Rights of Way Act of 2000, opens up new routes to walkers that may have previously been closed off, adding to existing rights of access in the Lake District.

Under the Act, the public has new rights of access on foot to areas classified as open country (mountain, moor, heath and down) and registered common land for recreational use. The right does not extend to activities such as cycling, canoeing, horse-riding or camping, though existing rights may already be in place for these activities on some land.

There are other restrictions in the Act: for instance, walkers must not damage any wall, fence, hedge, stile or gate in exercising their right of access, certain types of land are exempt and landowners have the right to limit access temporarily.

As a National Park, the Lake District is also subject to tighter planning and land usage.

It is worth familiarising yourself with the legislation and what it means for walking in the area. The Ramblers' Association can provide more details through their website (www.ramblers.org.uk/freedom).

Glossary

Common Cumbrian and northern English terms found in the text and maps:

band	ridge of a fell
beck	stream
bield	shelter
comb, combe, cove	mountain hollow
dale	valley
dodd, dod	rounded fell
fell	mountain; hill
force	waterfall
ghyll, gill	steep ravine
hause	saddle; pass
how	a low fell
knott	craggy fell
links	crags
mere	lake
moss	moorland
pike	pointed and rocky mountain
rake	a steep path in a gully or tilted shelf
rigg	ridge
scar	bare crag
scarth	notch in a ridge
slack	scree
spout	waterfall
stickle	sharp peak
tarn	small lake
thwaite	clearing; reclaimed wetland

Derwentwater and the Northern Fells

The Northern Fells beyond Skiddaw represent a huge area of rounded and peaty hills often neglected by walkers, but with plenty of interest, featuring dramatic gills and forces and, if you look for it, solitude. In contrast, on the southern side of the massif, Skiddaw and Blencathra flex their claw-crooked spurs towards Keswick, Lakeland's outdoors capital. This lively market town stands on Derwentwater, whose wooded shores lead you towards the rough mountains of popular Borrowdale.

In this section, five circuits take to the Northern Fells: a steep climb to the much-loved Blencathra contrasts with a short route to visit the hidden Bowscale Tarn; in the far north, a long and intricate circuit begins from Caldbeck; two routes begin from the centre of Keswick, one a varied journey over the high peak of Skiddaw, the other a short woodland amble to the top of Latrigg. Three routes start on the south side of Keswick: an adventure to the top of Eel Crag; a more unusual approach to High Spy; and, finally, a long hike that frequents the many teashops of Borrowdale.

1 **Saddleback ride from Threlkeld** 8
Challenging ascent of the celebrated Blencathra, rewarded by great views and a delightful return by waterfalls

2 **The Bannerdale Crags to Bowscale** 10
Half-day walk on the contrasting terrain of Bannerdale Crags and Bowscale Fell

3 **Oddfellows Knott** 12
Rough ground and a snaking gill make for a varied route in the Caldbeck Fells. Keen navigation is a must

4 **Latrigg Loop from Moot Hall** 14
Short walk from the centre of Keswick to climb one low fell with views over Derwentwater and Borrowdale

5 **Beyond Skiddaw** 16
Entertaining ascent of Skiddaw, with a rough approach by rocky watercourses and a long return under Lonscale Fell

6 **Eel Crag by Tower Ridge** 18
Over magnificent country to climb one high peak by less-visited ridges, with tricky navigation and exposure

7 **High Spy Handover** 20
Exhilarating route across varied terrain with a steep climb to gain High Spy by a less-walked spur

8 **A Borrowdale Trek** 22
Long but mostly low-level circuit to climb a wild fell above Borrowdale, with good paths and one steep descent

Saddleback ride from Threlkeld

Blencathra (868m)

Walk time 4h40 Height gain 700m
Distance 12km
OS Maps Explorer OL5 and OL4

**Steep but exhilarating climb up a real
Lake District favourite with an intricate
return on tracks and paths.**

Start from the telephone box and bus
shelter at the east end of Threlkeld
(GR324254). (Large parking area just over
the A66.) Walk northeast along Fell Side for
400m to a track on the left, marked as a
bridleway, to Gategill. Follow this track past
farm buildings and straight on at several
junctions to a gate near the water. A path
takes you through the trees from the gate,

exiting by a second gate to open ground.
Ford the gill and walk eastwards alongside
the fell wall for about 800m, crossing
Doddick Gill to rise steeply for a further
100m until the path divides. Leave the wall
here to climb north along Doddick Fell. This
gives a pleasant but fairly tough ascent,
without scrambling, to reach the main east
ridge of Blencathra and its fine views
beyond. For an interesting alternative to the
wide path up the ridge, make a fairly level
traverse into the combe for about 300m to
reach a small gill that feeds into Scales
Tarn. Enter the upper part of the ravine and
climb alongside the watercourse before
ascending a steep slope of clumpy grass to
bring you onto the plateau: it is now just a

short walk to the summit (GR323277) (2h40). Follow the ridge southwest to the next top, with its spectacular views of the northern Lakes. Drop northwest over easy grass slopes to reach the delightful Roughten Gill and accompany this downstream: the two waterfalls are best avoided on the north side. On reaching a track, turn south and watch for a path on the right after about 80m. This drops towards Glenderaterra Beck and a lower track overlooking Brundholme Wood (a brilliant display of colour in autumn), which is followed easily to the end of the road that serves Derwentfolds. Take a signposted path immediately on the left that zigzags up through fields to the Blencathra Centre. Walk between the buildings and up to the end of the road. Follow the road east for 400m and watch for a footpath on the right, which leads across farmland and back to the village of Threlkeld (4h40).

Lakeland cake

For fell food rich in energy, nothing can match the local Cumbrian confectionery. Joseph Wiper began production of Kendal Mint Cake in 1869 after a chance discovery. His sweet cake has supplied famous expeditions, including Shackleton's polar travels in 1914-17 and the first ascent of Everest in 1953: during the latter, Sherpa Tenzing left a piece on the summit to please the Gods. The calorific value of Romney's Kendal Mint Cake is 350kcal per 100 grams with no fat. For those with a sweet tooth still to spare, Sarah Nelson's Original Gingerbread is produced in Grasmere on the site of the old village school, by St Oswald's Church, and has been made here since 1854. Visitors should watch out for imitations, as only wrappers that claim 'None Genuine Without Trade Mark' contain the real thing. One slice is roughly equal to two points on the Weight Watchers scale.

◄ Looking to Skiddaw along Roughten Gill

The Bannerdale Crags to Bowscale

Bowscale Fell (702m)

Walk time 3h40 Height gain 500m
Distance 10km OS Map Explorer OL5

**Shorter route with steep ground in
ascent, rewarded by good views of
Blencathra, and easy access and return
by paths and tracks.**

   Start at the public telephone, close to the
Mill Inn, in the village of Mungrisdale
(GR362304). Take the track west from the
main road (marked as a footpath to
Mungrisdale Common), passing the house
of Bannerdale View to reach a gate. Go
through this and follow the track beyond,
heading directly towards The Tongue. Cross
a beck by the small footbridge after 500m
to gain a junction about 50m further on.
Take the left fork to wander southwest

along the River Glenderamackin by a good
footpath. After 1km, cross another beck and
watch for a path immediately beyond this
on the right, which climbs steeply up the
embankment and follows the prominent
east ridge. Where the spur steepens by the
remains of mine workings, traverse
southwards for about 200m (rather than
continue straight up): this entertaining
diversion cuts across a deep gully and
passes under a vegetated crag. Beyond this,
the terrain is steep but there are a number
of ways through low crags and up corners to
reach easy ground and the top of
Bannerdale Crags. Walk northwest and then
north on a good path to enjoy views of
Sharp Edge, Blencathra's celebrated
scramble, before climbing gentle slopes to
the summit of Bowscale Fell (GR333306)

◀ Up the River Caldew from the track to Bowscale Tarn

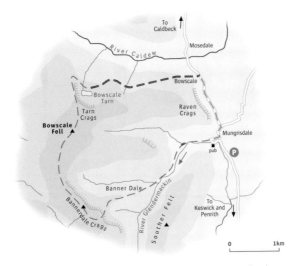

(2h20). Follow the plateau northeast for 400m, then descend NNW along the escarpment and above the steep and broken buttresses of Tarn Crags. Keep to this until it divides and you are level with the rough jewel of Bowscale Tarn. Contour under broken crags, and make your way to the water's edge. Descend eastwards by a good path: this soon becomes a gravel track and leads to Bowscale. Walk south along the road back to Mungrisdale and welcome refreshments at the start (3h40).

Eyes of the mountain

Bowscale Tarn sits in a north-facing amphitheatre of crags and receives little sunlight, making it an ideal home for the two immortal talking trout which, according to local legend, live in its depths. Unlike lakes, which are formed by valley glaciers, tarns are formed by small corrie glaciers and are roughly circular rather than long and thin. According to the artist W Heaton-Cooper, author of the classic *The Tarns of Lakeland* (1960), tarns are 'the eyes of the mountain' which allow them expression.

11

Oddfellows Knott

High Pike (658m), **Knott** (710m)

Walk time 6h Height gain 600m
Distance 17km OS Map Landranger 90

Long but pleasant walk with an intricate approach through farmland, requiring good route-finding skills. This circuit contains some boggy sections higher up and a river crossing on return.

Start at the Oddfellows Arms in the centre of Caldbeck (GR324397). Walk west along the road towards Upton. Turn left after about 150m to pass a row of cottages, and go through a gate on the right hand side of Hodden Court to reach a path. This takes you through trees, over a field, across a track and to the far left corner of another field. Walk east through two further fields to pass through a gate on the right by a house and track. Continue east along the track and the road with which it merges to a turning for Hudscales Farm (15 min). At the steading, cross the farmyard and walk clockwise around the house to reach a gate out to the open fell. Bear south over grassland to a shallow dip and a grassy track, which leads you southeast into an old mining area. To keep the slag heaps out of sight, tramp east over the wasteland and climb West Fell over clumpy grass. Then bear west and join a track by a number of sheltered hollows. Rather than follow the

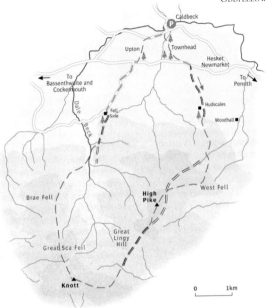

main track, climb High Pike directly to its summit (GR318350) (2h40). Descend off the top to rejoin the track and continue south under Great Lingy Hill and above Grainsgill Beck to Coomb Height. Walk easily west to the top of Knott (GR296330) (4h). Descend northwest over easier ground to Great Sca Fell. Drop down on the north side to find a grassy track and follow this northwards, taking every right turn to keep your height. When close to Brae Fell, descend north on easy slopes to reach a snaking gill east of Willy Knott. Drop into this fine feature and follow it to Dale Beck. Accompany the river downstream for about 500m before the

rough path guides you across the river (no bridge), below a pylon on the opposite bank. A short climb takes you to the gravel track above, which leads north to a gate and collection of farm buildings at Fell Side. Keep east of the buildings to reach a road, and follow this northeast (or take marked paths through the fields) to a T-junction after 1.5km. Turn right, watching for a stile on the left after 50m. Climb over this to walk north along the field by a wall, crossing this at another stile. Go through a gate on the left and descend through this next field to reach the road at Upton, just a short stroll from the start (6h).

◄ Knott and the Uldale Fells from the west

13

Latrigg Loop from Moot Hall

Latrigg (368m)

Walk time **2h** Height gain **250m**
Distance **8km** OS Map Explorer OL4

Intricate route on good footpaths and tracks, which returns through dense woodland by the River Greta.

Start at Moot Hall (information centre) in Keswick (GR265234). Walk a short way along Main Street and down one of the narrow ginnels on the right (north) to the car park. Cross the street beyond, and follow Otley Road for about 60m to a lane on the left: take this to swing right and cross the River Greta by a footbridge. Pass diagonally left over Fitz Parks to a small building, where a footpath leads northwest along a line of trees to Briar Rigg. Turn right along this and watch for a bridleway on the left after 150m: this carries you over the dual carriageway and through the gate directly ahead to enter woodland. Follow the track as it climbs first steeply and then more gradually around the hill, ignoring three minor turnings on the right. Pass through a gate to reach an interpretive sign where, just beyond on the right, a grassy path climbs the hill. Take this to meet a soft track that doubles back south and passes over the summit of Latrigg, giving fine views of Derwentwater and the Newlands Valley (1h) (GR280247). Descend

eastwards, passing through a gate to enter lush fields. Follow the escarpment for a time before dropping north beside the plantation to pick up a muddy track, which steers you through two gates to a road beyond. Turn right along the road, watching for a path on the left after about 300m. This wanders through dense trees to reach the River Greta, where a narrow, sculpted path leads you high above the raging froth downstream. Pass under the soaring

roadbridge to reach a junction at the Forge. Rather than cross the river, continue straight on along a track to Windebrowe and a road. Walk west on the road for about 150m to a turning on the left and a well-marked footpath. Follow this through woodland down to Keswick Bridge. Turn left under the old railway bridge, and follow the road around or walk through Fitz Parks to return to the town centre (2h).

The Old Railway

The former Cockermouth, Keswick and Penrith Railway, which closed to trains in 1972, included 78 bridges on the Keswick to Penrith section of which eight crossed the River Greta between Threlkeld and Keswick. The Lake District National Park Authority today maintains much of the trackbed as a scenic footpath, although there is a growing movement by local rail enthusiasts to re-open the line as a modern railway.

◀ Derwentwater and the Derwent Fells from Latrigg

Beyond Skiddaw

Skiddaw (931m)

Walk time **6h20** Height gain **900m**
Distance **18km** OS Map Explorer **OL4**

Stamina is required for this long and varied walk, with a gentle start along the River Derwent leading to much rougher terrain, an easy descent over grassy slopes and a long walk back to the centre of Keswick.

Start at Moot Hall (information centre) in Keswick (GR265236). Walk down Main Street, straight on at the roundabout and over the bridge by the Pencil Museum. Turn left immediately after the bridge, and follow a footpath towards Portinscale to reach a minor road. Turn left and walk across the footbridge over the River Derwent to pass through a gate on the right. From here, a path takes you along the river, and over many stiles, crossing the first roadbridge and ducking under the second, before ambling across fields to a gate at High Stock Bridge. Go through the gate and turn right along the track to reach the A591. Turn left and walk west for 300m to a minor road on the right, signposted for Millbeck and Applethwaite. After about 1km, this comes to Millbeck where a path on the left directs you towards Skiddaw: pass through two gates to enter open ground. For a slightly different approach to the peak, take the path that heads northeast, keeping just above the trees

before shadowing the west bank of Slades Beck. This path gives out higher up, but the route along the watercourse is quite straightforward. At the confluence of two tributaries, head northwards to follow Tongues Beck: in most conditions the lower reaches are quite dry and rocky but make for a rough climb as they steepen up. Leave the water in the steep upper combe to climb northeast along a grassy rib: this deposits you on the plateau between Little Man and Skiddaw. Walk northwest along the fence to meet the main

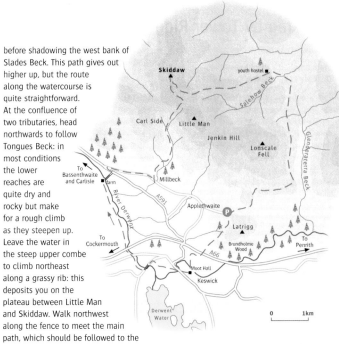

path, which should be followed to the summit of Skiddaw (GR260291) (3h20). [Variant from Millbeck: take the wide path up Carl Side. This path would also be the best escape from the summit.] Retrace your steps to the fence before Little Man. Pass through the gate, but leave the path to head ENE over easy-angled slopes where you can pick up a grassy track which leads over the top of Sale How and down to the youth hostel at Skiddaw House. Take a trail southwards to a junction above

Glenderaterra Beck, and carry straight on to climb gradually under the austere Lonscale Crags. Now contour around the hill to reach the car park by Latrigg. Leave by a path that drops west around this hill and becomes a track as it descends through the trees. Pass over the dual carriageway to the road at Briar Rigg. Turn right and pass through a gate on the left after 120m to enter Fitz Parks. Walk through the park and cross the river to return to the town centre (6h20).

◀ Skiddaw and Derwentwater from High Lodore

Eel Crag by Tower Ridge

Eel Crag (Crag Hill) (839m)

Walk time 5h40 Height gain 800m
Distance 15km OS Map Explorer OL4

**Fine circuit that starts along the
Coledale Valley and climbs Eel Crag by
quiet ridges, with a pleasant return by
Newlands Beck. This route contains
steep sections and minor exposure: a
good head for heights is a must.**

Start at the Royal Oak in the centre of
Braithwaite (GR231236). Walk along the
road for the Whinlatter Pass until you are
about 200m beyond the stone bridge,
where the road bends north and starts to
climb. Take the second footpath on the left,
marked for Coledale Hause, which rises
through the trees and soon meets a track.
Follow the track above Coledale Beck
towards the splendid Low Force. When you

are near the waterfall and extensive mine
workings, cross the stepping stones and
climb by the track for a further 1km until
the ground levels out below the daunting
bulk of Eel Crag. Instead of continuing to
Coledale Hause, leave the main track to
test your mountain skills. A beck can be
followed south over clumpy grass until,
after 300m, you find yourself directly below
the central rocky spur, midway between the
north ridge and Scott Crag. Climb southwest
over rounded, heathery terrain that soon
becomes craggy. The spur can be taken
directly with some easy scrambling over a
series of rocky steps. Alternatively, the
minor difficulties can be avoided with the
use of slight detours on the left side,
although it is best to return to the apex
every time. The ridge culminates in the
summit plateau, a short distance from the

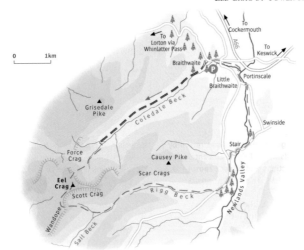

top of Eel Crag (GR193204) (3h). Drop easily SSW and rise gently south to the small cairn at the top of Wandope Moss. Take the majestic east ridge towards Addacomb Beck: the descent is particularly steep for the first 20m and then continues at a uniform angle. Descend almost all of the way to the valley to reach a clear path, which takes you eastwards and over the combe. Ignore a path that climbs to the left and instead drop gradually, keeping above Rigg Beck to reach the road at a single house. Follow the road northwards until it forks after about 1km. Take the right branch and descend through Stair, crossing two bridges. At the next fork beyond the hamlet, turn left towards Swinside and watch for a path on the left, immediately after a wood. This leads along the east bank of Newlands Beck to Little Braithwaite. Cross the roadbridge to the farm and watch for another footpath, which starts between the first shed and the farmhouse above. After 400m on the west bank, cross the beck by the footbridge, and pass through the caravan park into Braithwaite (5h40).

Mining at Force Crag

Abandoned in 1991, Force Crag was the last working metal mine in the Lake District. In a spectacular setting, the site was mined by various companies for lead from 1839 to 1865, and for zinc and barytes from 1867. Traces of the tracks, tramways and the aerial ropeway which transported material down Coledale Beck at various times can still be seen, but the mine-head buildings are now delapidated and entry to them is prohibited.

◀ Wandope and the Buttermere Fells from Eel Crag

High Spy Handover

High Spy (650m)

Walk time **5h** Height gain **800m**
Distance **13km** OS Map Explorer **OL4**

An unusual and varied circuit that involves two ascents, including a steep and less-visited ridge, and returns by good woodland paths.

Start at the lovely hamlet of Grange in Borrowdale (GR253174). Walk westwards through the village and take the Swinside road north. Watch for two paths on the north side of the ivy-covered house at Manesty. Take the more prominent trail (second on the left) that contours towards a plantation, before rising gradually to Hause Gate, just south of Cat Bells. Descend west

into the bowl under High Crags towards Little Town (alternative start point). Just above the farm, join a grassy track that contours southwards towards the craggy ridge of Castle Nook, a huge crooked thumb pressing onto the valley floor. Follow the track up the dale for 2.5km until you reach several slag heaps, where you should leave the track and start your ascent. After passing a cave (good shelter in rain), climb steep grassy steps towards broken crags until you are just below a rocky corner. Trend leftwards to avoid this, following the easiest ground. Now, keeping to an old section of wall, walk over gentle ground towards more crags. Breach these by making zigzags on the right-hand side.

◄ Looking south to the Borrowdale Fells

Rough heathery slopes constitute the upper half of the spur and provide a tough climb to reach the main ridge. Walk easily south to reach the summit of High Spy (GR234162) (3h40). [Variant: from Hause Gate, follow the ridge easily via Maiden Moor.] Descend grassy slopes to a wide combe. On the east side, pass over a stile to join a path just beyond which drops steeply east along the south bank of Tongue Gill and through old quarry works. Ignore the path for Rigg Head climbing hut, and continue to a junction of paths below a fence. Ford the gill here and join a grassy track in its gradual northeasterly descent to meet the Allerdale Ramble. Follow the trail northwards through inspiring craggy terrain and into woodland to reach the River Derwent. Keep to the path close to the river to reach a road by a campsite. Turn right and walk into Grange for tea and cakes (5h).

Map labels:
To Portinscale
Cat Bells ▲
To Buttermere
Little Town
Derwent Water
To Keswick
Manesty
P
Grange
Castle Nook
Nitting Haws
High Spy ▲
To Honister Hause
Rigghead Quarries
0   1km

Derwentwater

Often referred to as 'The Queen of the Lakes', this photogenic lake is surprisingly shallow: local roe deer have been known to swim over to Lord's Island on the lake. As well as its permanent islands, Derwentwater also has a 'ghost' island which appears in the southwest corner every few years. Caused by a build-up of marsh gases, the floating mass of vegetation was associated with many local superstitions and legends in years past.

A Borrowdale Trek

Great Crag (445m)

Walk time 6h20 Height gain 500m
Distance 20km OS Map Explorer OL4

What this circuit lacks in height it makes up for in distance, and walkers may be glad of the several teashops along the way. Care should be taken on the descent from Great Crag.

Start at the National Trust Car Park in Great Wood, below Walla Crag (GR272213). From the car park, a wide path leads south through the wood, crossing a forest track after 300m to reach Cat Gill. Cross the gill by the incredibly narrow bridge, descend a short way and continue southwards by the path to traverse under Falcon Crag. At a junction, choose the path on the left (marked for Ashness Bridge) and continue through bracken to meet a minor road at the bridge. Follow the road uphill to a wide path on the right, about 300m beyond a well-promoted viewpoint. This leads you through woodland, passes through a gate and crosses Watendlath Beck by a footbridge. Follow the beck on its west bank towards Watendlath Farm and teashop. From the footbridge just before the farm, walk along the west shore of the tarn for 100m to a junction. [Escape: take the right branch and descend directly to Rosthwaite, picking up the route further on.] Take the left branch to reach double gates, passing through the gate on the

right to follow the path beyond. Ford a beck and follow this upstream for 200m until signs direct you southwards across quaggy ground. From here, climb steeply by stone steps to the wildly undulating plateau. Make a short detour off the main path to the double-headed summit of Great Crag (GR268146) (2h40). Continue around the reed-choked waters of Dock Tarn to descend easily to Lingy End. Here the path, a winding slate staircase, steepens considerably and can be slippery. Pass through a gate to shortly climb a stile over the wall on the right, where a grassy path brings you onto the popular Cumbria Way. Head downstream on this, crossing the second bridge after 1km to enter Rosthwaite. Turn left into the village and take the first road on the right. Walk west past the Flock Inn and cross the River Derwent, where the path closest to the water meanders through High Hows Wood to reach a road by a campsite. Turn right and walk into Grange (where there is another teashop). Turn left to take the Swinside road north. After 1km, just before an oak tree in a field, take the path on the right. This leads over farmland and across the head of Derwentwater by boardwalks to reach a footbridge. Cross the bridge and take the path south to rejoin the road by High Lodore

Hotel. Turn left to High Lodore Farm and after turning off to the farm, follow a path behind the tearoom towards Shepherds Crag. About 50m from the crags, start to climb straight up by a path through the trees. Pass close to a waterfall and turn right at the junction to reach a gate. This lets you back to Watendlath Beck at the first bridge. Retrace your steps back to Great Wood (6h20).

◄ Rowling End and Grisedale Pike from Barrow Bay on Derwentwater

23

Ullswater and the Eastern Fells

Although it is the mountains that capture the walker's imagination, they are inseparable from the water features that give the Lake District its name. These lakes, elegantly reclining between the various massifs, provide every type of watersport from canoeing to sailing and wind-surfing. Ullswater lies at the centre of an area dominated by deep combes and steep ridges, such as High Street, but as you journey further east beyond Haweswater the mountains lose definition. Wherever you go, the becks and gills add interest to a hard climb while the quiet beauty of high mountain tarns reward.

This section kicks off with a steep gill climb to reach the Dodds above Thirlmere, while a tour of Helvellyn from Lanty's Tarn takes in two waterfalls. Another walk embarks from the Brothers Water in Patterdale. There are two jaunts from Ullswater: one makes waves to Howtown by steamboat; the other begins with a lakeside stroll towards Fusedale. Small Water Beck guides you from Haweswater to High Street, and the swampy ground above Swindale leads to Forces Falls. The last route takes you to Kentmere Reservoir from Troutbeck.

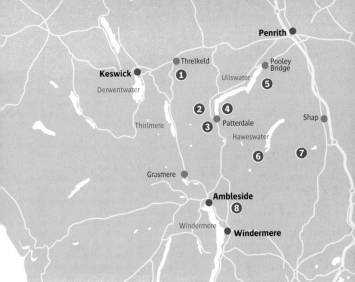

1 **Lap of the Dodds** 26
Quiet walk following a series of cascades and the undulating ridge of the Dodds, with an off-path ascent

2 **To Helvellyn and back** 28
Ascent of Helvellyn that offers an alternative to the main routes, with fewer difficulties and no scrambling

3 **Dove Crag by Brothers Water** 30
Hart Crag and Dove Crag, reached from a less-visited dale, with steep ascent and tricky route finding

4 **Ullswater Passage** 32
Voyage by steamer to climb Hallin Fell and Place Fell, rewarded with great views over Ullswater

5 **Pooley Bridge to Loadpot Hill** 34
Lakeside approach to a high circuit around Fusedale with a quick march by the Roman Road to return

6 **Haweswater and High Street** 36
Adventure along an undulating ridge to climb High Street and other smaller peaks. Sharp navigation is essential

7 **A Swindale Round** 38
Good fell-running circuit with an approach through Swindale to climb a rounded top in remote country

8 **The Yoke and the Bell** 40
Rewarding trek over the quieter fells of Kentmere Common, with lots of ascent, mild exposure and fine views

Lap of the Dodds

Stybarrow Dodd (843m),
Great Dodd (857m), **Clough Head** (726m)

Walk time **5h40** Height gain **800m**
Distance **15km** OS Map Explorer **OL5**

Fine ridge walk which rises steeply to traverse several rounded fells, returning by St John's Beck and green pastures.

Start by the telephone box in the village of Legburthwaite, at the foot of Thirlmere (GR318189). (Parking here and further north.) Walk east up the farm road for 100m to a junction by four garages. Take the left fork to the bend in the road after 120m, just before Stanah. Cross the stile directly ahead and walk up through the field, over another stile and easily up to meet Stanah Gill. Walk over the bridge and follow the path

(marked for Swirls) on the upper side of the fell wall until you reach another footbridge after about 500m. Climb along the north bank of Fisherplace Gill from here, passing many fine waterfalls and pools. The ascent becomes rockier but presents no difficulties, soon leading to gentler ground where the views open up. Continue beside the water, passing an old ruin, to the point where Brund Gill and Sticks Gill meet. Ford the latter and follow a short fin-like moraine by the remains of an old path. When this ends, continue over the extensive grassy slopes that overlook the steep ravine to reach level ground and a wide path just short of Sticks Pass. [Escape: follow the bridleway westwards down to Legburthwaite.] From the col, climb north on a renovated path to

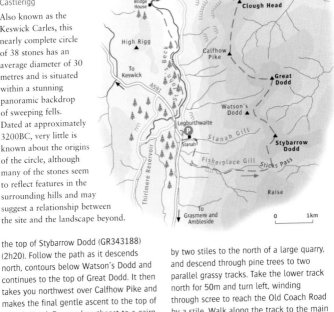

◄ Clough Head and the Dodds from the Castlerigg Stone Circle

Castlerigg

Also known as the Keswick Carles, this nearly complete circle of 38 stones has an average diameter of 30 metres and is situated within a stunning panoramic backdrop of sweeping fells. Dated at approximately 3200BC, very little is known about the origins of the circle, although many of the stones seem to reflect features in the surrounding hills and may suggest a relationship between the site and the landscape beyond.

the top of Stybarrow Dodd (GR343188) (2h20). Follow the path as it descends north, contours below Watson's Dodd and continues to the top of Great Dodd. It then takes you northwest over Calfhow Pike and makes the final gentle ascent to the top of Clough Head. Descend northeast to a cairn at White Pike, a small outcrop, and drop northwest from here into a grassy bowl. Contour around the bowl, skirt around a blunt rib and then continue under the Red Screes. Walk west through an area of small mounds to join a good path on its easy westerly descent, with views of the wild Wanthwaite Crags. Cross a wall and a fence

by two stiles to the north of a large quarry, and descend through pine trees to two parallel grassy tracks. Take the lower track north for 50m and turn left, winding through scree to reach the Old Coach Road by a stile. Walk along the track to the main road, and turn left. Take a well-signposted path on the right after 150m, which leads across fields to St John's Beck. Cross the river by the large farmhouse and walk upstream, following the path as it crosses fields, rejoins the beck at Sosgill Bridge and continues out to the A591, close to Legburthwaite and the start (5h40).

To Helvellyn and back

Helvellyn (950m), **Raise** (883m)

Walk time 6h40 Height gain 950m
Distance 18km OS Map Explorer OL5

A climb up one of the Lake District's big peaks by a less-visited spur. This route bypasses Striding Edge and Swirral Edge to minimise difficulties and provide a quieter and enjoyable journey.

Start at the bridge in the centre of Glenridding (GR386169). Walk west on a minor road which leads along the south bank of Glenridding Beck, passing shops and the village hall to reach a junction after 350m. Take the left fork to Westside, leaving the house to climb through the trees on a good path. Enter open country

and perform a large zigzag to reach Lanty's Tarn by Keldas. Skirt along the west bank of the tarn, before descending southwest into Grisedale to meet a wall with two gates. A path leads straight ahead from the upper gate, maintaining height above the valley floor towards Grisedale Hause. Leave the path after about 3km at Ruthwaite Lodge, and climb steeply west over rough ground, keeping left of the forces. Where the terrain eases, traverse south to Spout Crag, then turn to climb the ridge fairly directly. This involves several steep grassy terraces before a lull in the gradient. An ascent of The Tongue is next: a fine spur of grass and rock that holds no surprises and leads directly to the summit of Dollywaggon Pike.

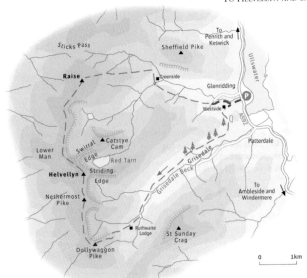

[Escape: descend southeast via the zigzags to Grisedale Hause.] Follow the wide path northwards over Nethermost Pike to the summit of Helvellyn (GR342152) (3h40). Continue along the ridge to Lower Man and over Whiteside Bank to the top of Raise. Drop east over easy slopes to a ruined chimney and the end of an old quarry track, which leads to a path at the edge of the hanging valley by Lucy's Tongue. Follow the path as it plunges in a series of sharp zigzags to Glenridding Beck. Cross the water by the footbridge, and take a path on the south side. At a fork after about 500m, bear left to accompany a wall to a gate. Pass through this, and follow tracks towards Rattlebeck Bridge. Take the track on the right before the bridge to pass the campsite and make the easy return into Glenridding village (6h40).

The Weatherman

One of the most unusual jobs in the Lake District National Park is that of Felltop Assessor. In order to issue weather information someone has to climb Helvellyn, one of the four highest peaks in the Lakes, every day of the year with an anemometer to take various weather readings. Despite the apparent difficulties, the last time the post was advertised more than fifty hardy souls applied.

◀ Striding Edge, St Sunday Crag and High Street from Helvellyn

Dove Crag by Brothers Water

Hart Crag (822m), **Dove Crag** (792m)

Walk time 4h40 Height gain 700m
Distance 13km OS Map Explorer OL5

A walk through two deep dales to a high combe, returning under the vertical walls of Dove Crag. Good navigation skills are required.

Start at Cow Bridge, just north of Brothers Water and west of Hartsop (GR403134). Take the marked path on the west side of the road that leads through the trees to Deepdale Bridge (short section of road walking). From the north side of the bridge, follow a walled track west to Lane Head. Turn left through a gate, where a grassy track takes you south towards Deepdale Hall Farmhouse. Avoid the farm by a gate on the right and continue SSW on a good track which, after passing Wall End, becomes a path out to open fell. Follow this path on the north bank of Deepdale Beck for a further 2km until it starts to climb towards Deepdale Hause. Leave the path here to head WSW, crossing two gills. Climb the steep grass banks of The Forces and enter Link Cove, with its imposing walls of crags. Bear north, keeping close to the right-hand edge of Scrubby Crag, to ascend a mix of grassy slopes and easy-angled slabs. Breach a line of broken rock to arrive on the top of The Step, and follow this

incomplete spur easily to join the path on the main ridge. This drops southeast before rising to Hart Crag (GR368113) (2h40). Continue southeast to Dove Crag. From the summit, walk southeast for about 200m and then drop into a vague bowl on the northeast side. This brings you down into a complex land of folds and dips. Aim for Stand Crags, which appears as a huge grassy fin. Cross an old fence to gain the top of the escarpment, offering the best views of Dovedale and Dove Crag. Follow the arête northwards for a short way until it is easier to drop northwest back towards

Dove Crag and down to the beck. Cross the water to reach a good path on the north bank and follow the main branch, which keeps height above the valley, eastwards. Enter woodland by a gate where, after a delightful descent through the trees, a track can be joined by some sheds. Turn left to reach Hartsop Hall and a junction. Take the left branch, passing the farm on its west side and continuing easily alongside Brothers Water to reach Cow Bridge (4h40).

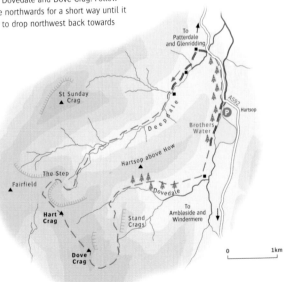

Ullswater Passage

Hallin Fell (388m), **Place Fell** (657m)

Walk time 4h20 Height gain 750m
Distance 11km OS Map Explorer OL5

Two peaks reached by mountain paths and some rougher ground, though no technical difficulty, with views over the lake and into the lovely Martindale. This route is accessed by the steamer from Glenridding.

Start at the Ullswater Steamer pier in Glenridding (GR390169). Take the boat one way to Howtown (GR443198) where, after leaving the jetty, turn right to cross a footbridge and follow a path, passing over two stiles, to reach a track. Turn right onto the track, pass through the gate on the left after 50m and take a path to a junction above the wood (5 min). Turn left to join the upper path on its gentle southerly climb until level with the road, overlooking a church. At this point, climb steeply north to the summit of Hallin Fell. Descend westwards by a vague trail that wanders in zigzags to the fell wall. An excellent path leads north to gain the lakeside path, which should now be followed through several gates to the hamlet of Sandwick. Walk up the road for 50m and turn onto the public bridleway to continue westwards for 1km to a footbridge at Scalehow Force. Leave the track here and climb along the east bank of

the waterfall over big rock steps. This is good fun and never difficult. [Variant: about 200m before the falls, a path rises through the bracken to easier ground.] At the top of the force, cross to the west side and begin an awkward ascent through the undergrowth to reach a cairn on the top of Low Birk Fell. Follow the high ground southwestwards over the undulating plateau. A short pull gets you to Birk Fell before alternating bumps and level boggy areas lead to the summit of Place Fell (GR405169) (3h20). Descend south by the main path to Boredale Hause, and take the lower of two paths that drop northwest towards the head of Ullswater. Pass through a gate to a

junction in the trees, and take the track on the right marked for Side Farm. When you reach a fork at the farm, turn left to follow a track to the road in Patterdale. Use the series of footpaths by the roadside to return to Glenridding pier (4h20).

Ullswater Steamers

Two of the three vessels that currently ferry thousands of visitors each year from Glenridding to Howtown and back were built by Thomas B Seath (1820-1903), one of the great Victorian Clydeside shipbuilders. A former cabin boy, Seath was inspired to become an engineer after playing with his pet white mouse in a toy wheel. His yard sent boats all over the world as well as building the famous 'Cluthas' which took daytrippers 'doon the watter' from Glasgow. The Clyde-built *The Lady of the Lake*, 1877, and *The Raven*, 1889, are joined in the winter months by the restored sea-launch *Lady Dorothy*, a former Guernsey ferry.

◄ A view along Grisedale to Place Fell

33

Pooley Bridge to Loadpot Hill

Steel Knotts (432m), **Loadpot Hill** (672m)

Walk time 6h Height gain 600m
Distance 18km OS Map Explorer OL5

**An intricate start to this long walk, with
two sharp ascents on good ridges and
excellent views of Ullswater throughout.**

Start in the centre of Pooley Bridge
(GR470244). Walk south on the track for
Eusemere Lodge, between the large car park
and the bridge over the River Eamont. Turn
right at the fork after 80m, pass through a
gate and head towards a boatyard where a
path leads along the banks of Ullswater to
Waterside House and campsite. Join the
road here and follow it for 500m, before
turning left to arrive at the farm and
campsite of Cross Dormont. Take the public
footpath around the farm and through fields
to reach Seat Farm. After passing these
buildings, follow signs around the edge of
two fields to reach Crookdyke. Walk along
the track for 200m, where a muddy path on
the left leads through gorse bushes to a
bridleway: ahead is an easy 2km stretch
under Auterstone Crag. On approaching
Howtown, take the left (main) fork to
continue to Mellguards. Follow the smart
gravel track for 50m, where there is a gate
on the left. Go through this to cross

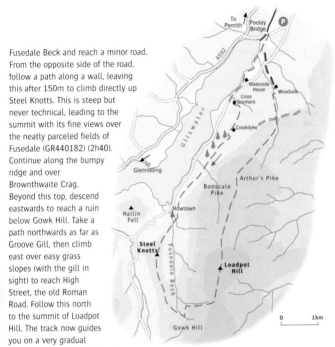

Fusedale Beck and reach a minor road. From the opposite side of the road, follow a path along a wall, leaving this after 150m to climb directly up Steel Knotts. This is steep but never technical, leading to the summit with its fine views over the neatly parcelled fields of Fusedale (GR440182) (2h40). Continue along the bumpy ridge and over Brownthwaite Crag. Beyond this top, descend eastwards to reach a ruin below Gowk Hill. Take a path northwards as far as Groove Gill, then climb east over easy grass slopes (with the gill in sight) to reach High Street, the old Roman Road. Follow this north to the summit of Loadpot Hill. The track now guides you on a very gradual northwards descent. At a junction after 2km, take the left fork to walk over Arthur's Pike. Drop gently northeast, crossing a large track by Aik Beck and continuing by a path through bracken on the west bank. Before reaching the plantation, ford the water and take the path to Woodside. Enter the caravan site and descend to the road. From here, there are a number of ways to return to Pooley Bridge and the start (6h).

Donald Campbell

On 23 July 1955 the remarkable Donald Campbell broke the existing world speed record on Ullswater in his turbo-jet hyrdoplane *Bluebird*, reaching an average speed of 202.32mph. He beat the record nine more times before losing his life attempting to break it yet again on Coniston Water in 1967.

◂ Approaching Howtown and looking westwards along Ullswater

35

Haweswater and High Street

High Street (828m)

Walk time **5h** Height gain **750m**
Distance **12km** OS Map Explorer **OL5**

A walk at the head of Haweswater Reservoir to climb a less-frequented spur with some route-finding interest and fantastic views of Helvellyn.

Start at the head of Haweswater Reservoir (GR468107). Walk through the gate by the bus stop (summer service only) and along the path to reach a junction after 60m. Continue straight on, following the bridleway towards Kentmere. This path climbs easily beside a series of cascades to reach Small Water. Cross the beck and, rather than follow the main path around the tarn, bear north beside giant boulders to ascend a steep grass slope to the east ridge

of Mardale Ill Bell, known as Piot Crag. Follow the spur with interest, avoiding steeper ground by keeping first to the north side and then to the south, to reach a crag with a large spill of scree below. This crag can be tackled on its right hand side up a short corner, or avoided with ease by contouring further right (north) at the level of the scree to grassy slopes. Climb over ragged sections of spoil and other reminders of former industry. Above this point, the ridge widens and leads easily to the top of Mardale Ill Bell. Follow the unmistakable path northwest until you encounter further Roman Road and an impressive wall that leads to the summit of High Street (GR441111) (2h20). Descend by the line of the wall to a prominent gap, and walk 60m up the other side to reach a cairn

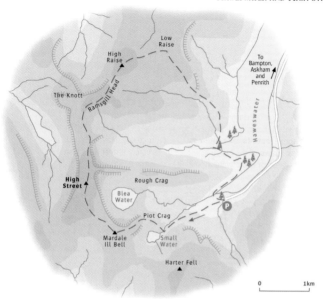

at a path junction. Take the path on the right to ascend Ramsgill Head with its great views into Martindale Common. A gentle descent and a short climb bring you to the top of High Raise: from here, bear ENE over the plateau to reach the cairn on the top of Low Raise. Rather than follow grassy tracks northwards, turn southeast where awkward and boggy terrain soon leads you to a good

ridge that drops in fits and starts. The ground steepens at Birks Crag but is never difficult. Descend through the lower bracken to gain the northeast corner of a plantation, whose wall should be followed anti-clockwise for some adventure. Join the excellent path below the forest and follow this southwards back to the head of Haweswater and the start (5h).

The lost village

The village of Mardale at the south end of Haweswater disappeared under water when the valley was flooded in 1935 in order to create a reservoir to provide the city of Manchester with a new water supply. When the water level is low, however, many of the ruined walls can be seen including those of the old local pub, the Dun Bull. Haweswater is also home to some notable birdlife: England's only breeding pair of golden eagles live here.

◀ Looking north along Haweswater Reservoir from The Rigg

A Swindale Round

Branstree (713m)

Walk time 5h Height gain 500m
Distance 17 km
OS Maps Explorer OL5 and OL7

Grassy tracks lead from the tranquil Swindale to a plateau with fine views of High Street. Bog is a feature on both the outward and return journeys, but there are no technical difficulties.

Start in Swindale, about 4km south of Bampton Grange (no parking south of GR522142 but several areas north). Walk southwest through this pleasant dale to reach Swindale Head after 2.5km. At the farmhouse, take the signposted Old Corpse Road on the right. This passes through two gates and climbs northwest up the broken

remains of an old track to reach the beck at another gate. Cross the beck, follow the wall to a large tree and double back to cross the water again at the top of a plantation: a grassy path now leads you southwest over easy slopes. Where the terrain flattens completely, at the start of a series of old posts, leave the main path and bear south along a faint trail to climb to the top of Selside. Accompany the fence on its descent through boggy ground and up to the top of Branstree, a journey with great views of High Street and Haweswater (GR478099) (2h40). Descend easily southwest to a gate at Gatescarth Pass. Go through this to follow the winding track southeast to Brownhowe Bottom, a complex folded area with the spoils and ruined

◄ Mosedale Beck by Swindale Common

buildings of former quarrying. Ford the beck and follow the signposted bridleway towards Swindale Head. A fairly boggy section takes you over the col and down to the comfortable mountain hut at Mosedale. Join the track here and follow it until, after about 600m, it turns south immediately after fording a small gill. Now leave the track to follow a narrow path that traverses at this level, keeping close to an old wall. After passing through a gate, where the views of Swindale open up once more, descend by switchbacks to the floor of the valley. [Detour: it is worth visiting Forces Falls, just a short way upstream.] A grassy track leads back to Swindale Head. Keep to a gated track on the west side of the farm and retrace your steps to the start (5h).

The Old Corpse Road

Alfred Wainwright described Swindale as a 'shy and beautiful little valley' and 'almost the only one remaining that does not cater for the motorist'. Before the motor car, however, villagers also often had to carry their dead over the fells to their place of burial. The Old Corpse Road was regularly used by the people of Mardale who carried coffins over Selside Pike into Swindale and on to Shap's churchyard for burial.

The Yoke and the Bell

Ill Bell (757m)

Walk time **7h** Height gain **900m**
Distance **20km** OS Map **Explorer OL7**

A steep and occasionally exposed adventure along an undulating ridge, with a long return by the old Roman Road of High Street.

Start at the Jesus Church in Troutbeck (GR413028). (Parking at Church Bridge or southwest of Town End.) Walk southwest over the bridge to a track on the left after 100m. Follow the stony Garburn Road past The Howe, switching back northeast to climb gradually to Garburn Nook. Descend on the main track towards Kentmere to reach houses and a junction. Take the grassy track, signposted for Kentmere Reservoir, which leads through a gate and shortly merges with a private road. Follow this easily north to Hartrigg Farm, passing through the gate on the left to avoid the farm. Continue past the steep Rainsborrow Crag, old quarry buildings and spoil heaps to reach the reservoir where you should leave the level ground and climb steeply southwest along a blunt rib to the boggy top of Steel Rigg. Traverse south around a cove to spoil and a quarried scoop. From this perspective the east ridge of Yoke looks wildly serrated and almost alpine, but this is an illusion. Make a leftwards

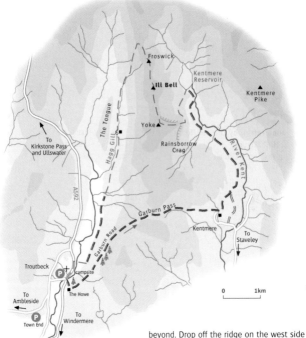

diagonal climb, crossing an old wall to gain the edge of the arête. Now ascend directly up the apex of the ridge, with exposed views over the dale. Grassy steps lead to a rocky section that can be easily avoided on the north side. Return to the arête to reach gentle, undulating ground and the top of Yoke. Join the main path and make the short journey north to the summit of Ill Bell (GR436077) (4h40). Descend north and continue over the top of Froswick to the col

beyond. Drop off the ridge on the west side to gain a grassy path that makes a pleasant descent: this is High Street, the old Roman Road. Pass through a gate and follow the wildly meandering Hagg Gill to a junction by an old quarry building. Pass through the gate on the left to cross the beck by the footbridge. Follow a muddy track on the east bank, passing Lowther Brow and the farm at Long Green Head to reach a fork. Take the path on the right to enter Limefitt Park. Pass through the campsite to the road, a short distance from your start point (7h).

◀ By Hagg Gill below The Tongue, looking north to Threshwaite Mouth

41

Grasmere, Langdale and Coniston

The canon of literature and poetry
inspired by the Lakes is nowhere more
celebrated than in this central area of the
Lake District. Wordsworth and Coleridge
lived in Grasmere, John Ruskin in Coniston,
and Beatrix Potter ran a farm above
Troutbeck. The landscape was their muse:
dense lakeside woodland, the staccato
sounds of the farm resonating in the clean
air and the hues of the fellside in constant
shift. Much of this appeal remains,
accounting for the area's enduring popularity.

Two contrasting walks in this section
begin from Grasmere: one tackles distant
Fairfield and the other the iconic Helm
Crag. Two half-day walks climb low fells,
one from Ambleside and the other from
Elterwater. A fun scramble leads to the
Langdale Pikes and a much longer journey
involves the high peaks of Bow Fell and
Crinkle Crags. Two routes begin at Coniston:
one passing the old Tilberthwaite quarries
to climb Wetherlam and the other makes
an unorthodox ascent of the Old Man.

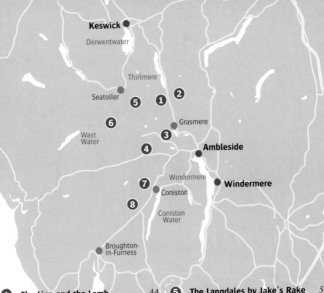

1 **The Lion and the Lamb** 44
Sharp climb up Helm Crag with an unusual traverse to reach the sparkling Easedale Tarn and nearby waterfalls

2 **Fairfield and St Sunday** 46
Less usual route to climb Fairfield and its smaller neighbours, with some steep though short-lived descents

3 **An Ambleside Ramble** 48
Scenic half-day walk from Ambleside, which ascends Loughrigg and returns by Grasmere and Rydal Water

4 **Lingmoor from Elterwater** 50
Compact route from Elterwater to follow a fine ridge with commanding views of the Langdale Pikes

5 **The Langdales by Jake's Rake** 52
Scramble up Jake's Rake to reach the Pikes. Consider taking a rope, and start early to avoid the crowds

6 **Bow Fell and Crinkle Crags** 54
Exposed traverse over Bow Fell and neighbouring peaks with steep sections. Good navigation is a must

7 **Quarries of Wetherlam** 56
Circuit of deep gorges, a narrow ridge and a complex peak, returning by an atmospheric and less-visited combe

8 **The Old man of Coniston** 58
Classic peak and a chain of tarns high above Coniston, with challenging steep and exposed ground

The Lion and the Lamb

Helm Crag (405m),
Calf Crag (537m)

Walk time 4h40 Height gain 700m
Distance 10km OS Map Landranger 90

**Explore the scenery around Grasmere
with a walk that starts at the centre of
the village to climb a long undulating
ridge and a much-loved peak.**

Start on Broadgate in Grasmere village
(GR336077). Head northwards on Easedale
Road (path beside the road), crossing Goody
Bridge to reach a junction. Take the left fork
past open fields to reach the hamlet of

Lancrigg. Continue on a track beyond the
first couple of houses to another junction,
this time turning right along a cobbled lane
to a gate. Pass through the gate, turn left
and watch for a path in the trees on the
right after 50m. Follow this as it climbs
north along old quarry steps. Zigzag over
the top of White Crag and make the final
push to the summit of Helm Crag: this is a
complex top of folds with several famous
outcrops, including the Lion and the Lamb.
Descend northwest on a steep path to
Bracken Hause, and continue on the rough
ridge over Gibson Knott. This involves

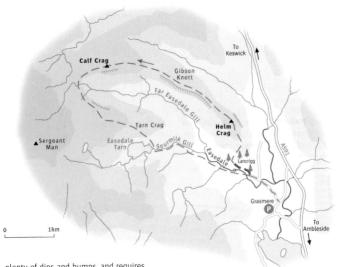

plenty of dips and bumps, and requires stamina to reach the low buttresses that line the top of Calf Crag (GR302104) (2h40). Descend south over grassy slopes to reach the Easedale path. [Escape: follow the path eastwards along the valley to Lancrigg.] Climb directly south on grassy slopes for about 150m in height until you are above the steep crags to the east. Traverse easily southeast along Deer Bields, following a natural terrace: this provides no technical

difficulty and reaches the east spur that descends from Tarn Crag. Drop east by a faint path for a short time before cutting down through the bracken to the foot of the peaceful Easedale Tarn. Cross the outlet and accompany the cascading Sourmilk Gill by an excellent path into Easedale. Follow the main path and cross Easedale Beck to leave just a short walk into Grasmere (4h40).

Cumberland wrestling

Grasmere has hosted an annual sports day featuring many traditional activities, including fell racing, track and field events and Cumberland wrestling, every August for more than 150 years. Introduced by the Vikings, wrestling has developed several local styles in England with different holds and rules. The Cumberland wrestling rules, for example, do not allow kicking, unlike the West Country style which allows the 'showing of the toe'.

◂ Gibson Knott from Deer Bields, Grasmere Common

Fairfield and St Sunday

Fairfield (873m), **St Sunday Crag (841m)**,
Steel Fell (553m)

Walk time 6h20 + detour 40 min
Height gain 1100m Distance 16 km
OS Maps Explorer OL7 and OL5

**This circuit starts by a gill to climb one
massif with another minor ascent on
return. There are some steep but fairly
short-lived sections in descent.**

Start in the centre of the village of
Grasmere (GR335075). Walk northeast
along Broadgate to emerge on the A591
opposite The Swan. Cross the main road and
proceed along the lane to the right of the
pub. Take the second turning on the right, a
narrow tarmac track signposted for
Greenhead Gill and Alcock Tarn. Where the

track swings to the left after 300m, pass
through the gate directly ahead and turn
right to cross the footbridge. Follow a good
path first by the south bank of the gill and
then up to reach an isolated plantation. At
the northeast corner of the trees, leave the
main path and take a smaller trail through
the heather to join Greenhead Gill again.
Walk upstream with interest: after some old
ruins, the path disappears but the journey is
never difficult. Higher up, grassy runnels fan
out from the water, now barely a trickle:
any one of these can be followed to meet
the path along the main ridge and up to the
top of Great Rigg. A main descent and
climb lead to Fairfield (GR359118) (3h).
From the northerly star-shaped shelter, walk
about 120m NNW to the start of the north

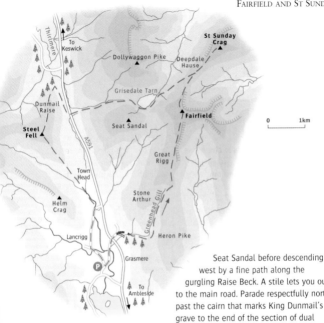

ridge. This makes for an awkward descent at first and it is best to keep west to avoid steeper ground. Continue over broken rock to a niche before Cofa Pike. Although the ridge is narrow here it gives no tricky sections to reach Deepdale Hause, shared with St Sunday Crag. [Detour: Climb northeast to the summit of St Sunday Crag. Return the same way (add 40 min).] Descend southwest from the gap by one of the many narrow paths that lead towards Grisedale Tarn. Keep to the south side of the tarn and climb to Grisedale Hause [Escape: descend Little Tongue to return to Grasmere village.] Traverse northwest under

Seat Sandal before descending west by a fine path along the gurgling Raise Beck. A stile lets you out to the main road. Parade respectfully north past the cairn that marks King Dunmail's grave to the end of the section of dual carriageway. Cross a stile on the west side of the road and take the bridleway towards Thirlmere, passing through one gate after 500m to another below a grassy field. Now turn to climb steeply beside a plantation along a blunt grassy rib, which provides fine views of the reservoir. Pass through a gate and climb onto the rougher slopes of Steel Fell where, after crossing a stile, the fence can be followed to the double-headed summit. Descend southeast by a slender path: this steepens into hairpins through broken crags but gives a pleasant descent down to the road at Helmside. Follow minor roads back into Grasmere (6h20).

◀ Fairfield from Helm Crag

An Ambleside Ramble

Loughrigg Fell (335m)

Walk time **3h20** Height gain **300m**
Distance **10km** OS Map Explorer **OL7**

A short walk on good paths with great views of the Langdale Pikes and the woods around Grasmere, returning through historic gardens.

Start at the cinema in the centre of Ambleside (GR374045). At the road junction immediately south of the cinema, take Vicarage Road towards Rothay Park. Pass St Mary's Church and walk through the park. Cross the river by a stone footbridge, and turn right along the road to a junction after 60m. Go left to climb steeply west along a private tarmac road to Brow Head. Follow the zigzag from the farm, ignoring the woodland path to Clappersgate, and continue west into open country by a stony track: this soon becomes a grassy path. After passing through three gates, the path drops to cross a beck and divides. Bear northwest and climb easily to a cairn on Black Mire: this gives a great vantage point to Loughrigg Tarn and Wetherlam beyond. Descend a short way and continue steadily to the summit of Loughrigg Fell (GR347052) (1h40). Drop northwest along the path: this is restored in most places and gives splendid views of the forests around Grasmere (especially when the trees are in

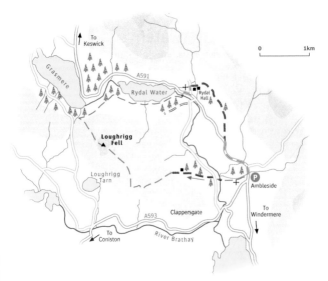

autumn colour). When you reach Loughrigg Terrace, turn right to contour eastwards. Take the left turn after 500m and a right turn at the next junction to drop down by a wall to Rydal Water. Walk along the south bank and enter private woodland to continue near the shore, crossing the River Rothay by the footbridge to emerge on the road directly opposite the pub. Cross the road and walk east to the first junction by the public telephone. Climb the hill past St Mary's Church, and take the track on the right after 250m for Rydal Hall. This passes the well-promoted tearoom, winding between the outbuildings of this historic hall to reach a junction and the start of open gardens. Turn left and follow the track through stately grounds to emerge on the road at Scandale Bridge. This leaves only a short walk back to Ambleside (3h20).

Rushbearing

When churches had earthen floors and parishioners were buried inside as well as out, wild rushes were gathered and used in many Cumbrian villages to freshen the air and provide some warmth in the winter months. Every summer, around St Oswald's Day (5 August), the people of Grasmere and Ambleside keep this old custom and, following a colourful parade around town, lay the 'rushbearings' in their churches.

◀ Grasmere and Dunmail Raise from Loughrigg Terrace

Lingmoor from Elterwater

Lingmoor Fell (469m)

Walk time **4h** Height gain **500m**
Distance **10km**
OS Maps **Explorer OL6 and OL7**

**A fairly short walk that follows good
paths and tracks to climb one low peak
with unbeatable views.**

Start at the bridge over Great Langdale
Beck in Elterwater (GR327047). Walk
northwest along the private road on the
south side of the river towards the quarry.
Watch for a path on the right after 300m,
opposite a large cave. Follow the water to
the bend in the river and cross by the
footbridge to reach the road. Pass the

Wainwrights Inn and take the footpath on
the left after 50m: this leads to a junction
by Thrang Farm. Go straight ahead on the
right side of a collection of buildings, and
continue along a walled footpath. This soon
joins a track, which is followed over the
river to the campsite. A track leads beside
the water to Oak Howe, where a path
continues behind the house and barn to a
junction. Take the northwest branch to
circumvent the impenetrable northern
slopes of Oak Howe Needle. Keeping above
Side House, aim for the plantation above
the Langdale campsite. Maintain your
height above the trees to gain a path
alongside a wall, which is followed uphill to

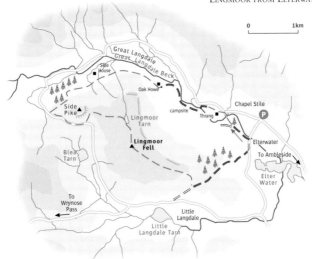

0   1km

gain the col and the road beneath Side Pike. Descend by the road overlooking Blea Tarn for about 300m and watch for a path on the left, which climbs steeply under Side Pike to reach a high wall. Now accompany the ridge eastwards and cross the wall by the stile. Rather than follow the heavily eroded highest ground, contour eastwards and make your way to the seclusion of Lingmoor Tarn. Twist your way over bumps and hollows to the top of Brown How, the summit of Lingmoor Fell (GR303045) (3h).

Descend ESE, keeping to the north side of the wall. The ridge is fairly undulated and gives great views of Wetherlam. Cross to the south side of the wall by a stile at a short section of fencing. Take the path that avoids the steep quarried cliffs to the north, leading you on past spoils and ruins. Follow the path southwards off the ridge just before an intersecting wall, and descend by zigzags to a track. Turn left to take the track past farmland and through woodland to Elterwater (4h).

Heather ale

Lingmoor Fell takes its name from ling, another name for common heather (*Calluna vulgaris*), which once covered the northern slopes of this fell. Evidence from archaeological digs has shown that ale made from 'the bonny bells' is believed to have been drunk since around 2000BC. After being revived by a Scottish brewery in 1992, 'Fraoch Leann' or Heather Ale has once again become popular with beer aficionados.

◀ Looking east along old quarry works on Lingmoor

The Langdales by Jake's Rake

Harrison Stickle (736m)

Walk time **4h40** Height gain **700m**
Distance **11km** OS Map Explorer **OL6**

An exciting circuit in one of the most popular areas of the Lakes, with a famous scramble and some exposure followed by a traverse of the Pikes on good paths. Non-scramblers can avoid the thrills of Jake's Rake altogether.

Start at the New Dungeon Ghyll Hotel and Stickle Barn (GR294065). Pass through the gate behind the inns to take the excellent path directly ahead, which climbs alongside the west bank of Stickle Ghyll.

This soon crosses the water and continues steeply, fording the beck again before arriving at the popular Stickle Tarn. It is worth spending a few minutes here to study the route ahead if you plan to climb Jake's Rake. Walk clockwise around the tarn to the far side. Climb over a delta of loose scree to the right of the lowest crags of Pavey Ark to reach the start of the rising diagonal rampline. Jake's Rake trends leftwards across the whole face at roughly 45°, providing a highly entertaining scramble which is enticing to start and becomes gradually harder. The first section climbs a wide and steep staircase, often

enclosed, and ends at the top of a pillar. There is a short level traverse before the crux, an awkward cracked block. A mixture of walking and scrambling leads to open slabs. There are many choices (all difficult) for ascending the slabs to reach the plateau, just southwest of the top of Pavey Ark. Follow the higher ground southwestwards to the summit of Harrison Stickle (GR281074) (2h40). [Variant to avoid scrambling: from the southwest tip of Stickle Tarn, take the path which rises in switchbacks to the plateau just north of Harrison Stickle.]

Drop WNW via the renovated path to a wide level col before a steep ascent to the rocky top of Pike of Stickle. Descend with care and trend north, then northwest, over the quaggy reaches of Martcrag Moor to Stake Pass. Join an excellent path to drop down Stake Gill to Mickleden. Take the grassy track eastwards to the Old Dungeon Ghyll Hotel. Enjoy the hospitality here or continue by road to a choice of venues at the start (4h40).

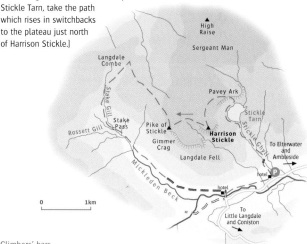

High Raise

Sergeant Man

Langdale Combe

Stake Gill

Pavey Ark

Stickle Tarn

Rossett Gill

Stake Pass

Pike of Stickle

Harrison Stickle

Stickle Ghyll

Gimmer Crag

To Elterwater and Ambleside

Langdale Fell

Mickleden Beck

hotel P

hotel

To Little Langdale and Coniston

0   1km

Climbers' bars

Situated about a mile apart, the Old and New Dungeon Ghyll Hotels are both welcoming to walkers coming off Langdale Fell. The older hotel also has a history of playing host to some of the most famous pioneering names in British climbing in the 1960s and '70s, including Chris Bonington, Joe Brown and Don Whillans.

◀ Harrison Stickle from Pike of Stickle

Bow Fell and Crinkle Crags

Bow Fell (902m), **Crinkle Crags** (859m), **Pike of Blisco** (705m)

Walk time **6h20** Height gain **1000m**
Distance **14km** OS Map **Explorer OL6**

A demanding route over multiple peaks, requiring plenty of stamina, a head for heights and keen navigation skills.

Start at the Old Dungeon Ghyll Hotel in Langdale (GR285061). Take the track behind the hotel northwestwards along Mickleden, where it becomes a path. When this divides after crossing Stake Gill, take the left branch to climb beside Rossett Gill. Continue along the path as it performs one small loop and then a much longer detour from the gill. When it doubles back again,

leave the well-laid steps to head diagonally southwards over rough grass towards the complex east face of Bow Fell. Climb over small boulders to the centre of the corrie below the monolith of Bowfell Buttress, keeping Great Slab/Cambridge Crag to your left. Ascend Easy Gully directly ahead either by the scree above or a series of steep grassy steps to the left. This reaches easy ground: the summit of Bow Fell is a short walk south (GR244064) (3h). For a different descent, return to the top of Easy Gully, and drop westwards over grassy slopes towards Yeastyrigg Gill. Where the terrain flattens out after about 400m, turn south to pass under the calved boulders of Slate Crag (which has a prominent X-shaped buttress

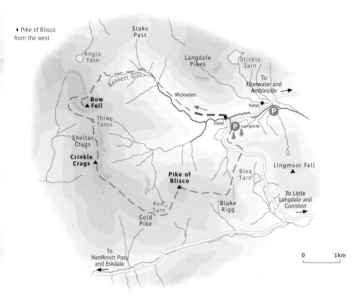

◄ Pike of Blisco
from the west

on its east side) on easy grass slopes. Traverse at this level under the screes of Bowfell Links to reach the Three Tarns. [Escape: descend east along The Band to Langdale.] Follow the ridge over the many lumps and dips that form Crinkle Crags. The summit is Long Top, the fourth in a series of rocky bumps. Drop steeply on the southwest side to avoid the bad step before climbing over a final top, which marks the end of the difficulties. Leave the main path and walk south to cross the temporary electric fence, then bear southeast over grassy slopes towards Cold Pike. Cross back over the fence near the top and walk over the confused summit, descending with care

past small outcrops to gain the head of Red Tarn. Launch straight up Pike of Blisco to its summit (GR272042) (5h). Descend east and march over the twisted ground of Wrynose Fell to reach Blake Rigg with its two competing high points, both bearing cairns. Descend northwards: this requires some clever thinking to choose the easiest ground of grassy ramps and gullies. Aim directly for Side Pike to gain the road at the top of the pass. Cross the stile ahead and drop northwards into Langdale. Pass through the end of the National Trust campsite and walk the short distance to welcome refreshment in the Old Dungeon Ghyll Hotel (6h20).

Quarries of Wetherlam

Wetherlam (762m)

Walk time **4h20** Height gain **700m**
Distance **12km**
OS Maps **Explorer OL6 (and OL7)**

A varied half-day route, starting with an easy trek through woodland and past old quarries to follow a footpath above a deep chasm and climb one rocky peak high above Coniston.

Start at the Ruskin Museum in the centre of Coniston village (GR302977). Walk north along the minor road at the rear of the museum and, where the road swings left after 300m to become a bumpy track, turn right to follow a well-built footpath. This leads pleasantly northeast through woodland above Far End to reach the A593 at the junction with the minor road to High Tilberthwaite. Walk up this road towards the hamlet to reach a car park surrounded by spoils from the old quarry (alternative start point). Climb the neat trail of slate steps from the south end of the car park to pass deep pits and contour above the dark chasm of Tilberthwaite Gill. Cross Crook Beck by stepping stones, and walk northwest to gain the lower bumps of Steel Edge. Climb southwest along the ridge: this is grassy and folded at first, but though it

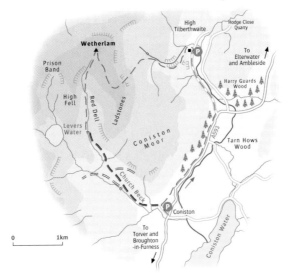

later becomes rocky and pronounced poses no real challenges to reach easier ground. Walk NNW for 1km on the undulating upper ridge to gain the summit of Wetherlam (GR288011) (3h). Descend southwards, making your way easily around low buttresses, to enter the fine U-shaped combe of Red Dell. On the steeper upper section, accompany a vague path on the east bank of the beck. Cross the water

where the terrain levels out and pass through a giant boulderfield to reach old mine workings. [Variant: for a longer challenge, join the next route (The Old Man of Coniston).] Cross the bridge here, pass the huge ruin and take an old grassy track southeast. At the junction that overlooks a row of cottages, turn right and descend to the track above Church Beck. Follow this track easily back into the village (4h20).

Swallows and Amazons

The result of spending many happy childhood summer holidays on a farm on the banks of Coniston Water, Arthur Ransome's classic *Swallows and Amazons* is an enduring tale of innocent adventure and discovery, still popular with adults as well as children. The locations which appear in the book are taken from various sites around the Lakes: Friar's Crag on Derwentwater, for example, became the lookout spot 'Darien' in the book, and The Old Man of Coniston became the mighty 'Kanchenjunga'.

◂ Wetherlam from the lower slopes of Lingmoor Fell

The Old Man of Coniston

The Old Man of Coniston (803m)

Walk time 4h40 Height gain 800m
Distance 12km OS Map Explorer OL6

Interesting setting for an unusual route up a popular peak, passing the remains of copper mines and slate quarries with a return through fields.

Start at the Ruskin Museum in the centre of Coniston village (GR302976). Walk north along the minor road at the rear of the museum: this soon becomes a bumpy track. Follow it to a junction 200m beyond the bridge over Church Beck, and take the right fork. Ignore a branch that serves a collection of houses, instead continuing to a T-junction below old quarries and spoils. Turn left here to make a rising diagonal above the valley, passing a ruined structure

to cross the bridge over Red Dell Beck. Follow some fencing past mine shafts and then take the obvious path on the left, climbing steeply west to join the top of Kennel Crag at a cairn. Wander along the grassy spur to Levers Water. Walk across the S-shaped barrage and then climb south on a path between fenced-off areas. When the path begins to descend to Boulder Valley, leave it to climb west on steep, grassy slopes towards the crags of Brim Fell. When you are directly beneath an intimidating spike, traverse southwards under the crags, crossing a patch of scree to start before following trails over fairly exposed ground. The difficulties are soon over and bumpy ground leads towards Low Water. [Variant: to avoid the traverse under Brim Fell, descend into Boulder Valley and

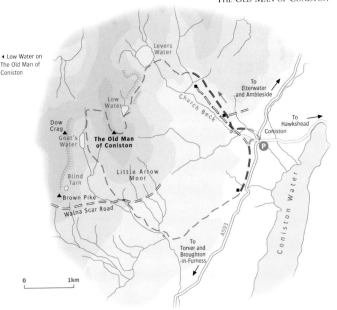

◄ Low Water on The Old Man of Coniston

walk across to Crowberry Haws. Then take the main path west to Low Water.] From this inviting tarn, use the main path that snakes up easily to gain the summit of The Old Man of Coniston (GR272978) (2h40). Walk NNW off the top for about 400m, then more westwards to reach Goat's Hause. Descend steeply by the path to dark Goat's Water, and walk southeast on easy ground to gain the prominent Walna Scar Road. Follow this track east for 80m to a path on the right. This leads southeast through the bracken, passing more remains of the area's industrial heritage to reach a path junction at a bridge. Continue straight on rather than crossing the beck, and pass through two gates to reach a signpost in the middle of a field. Turn east towards Park Gate, following a high wall up a slight incline. Use the stile to cross this wall where it turns abruptly, and continue east to join a good track by a gate and pylon on the far side of a small basin. This leads northeast and through a number of gates to the road. Walk down the hill towards Coniston and, after 100m, take the first turn on the left where signs indicate a permitted footpath to Coniston. This passes delightful cottages to reach Old Furness Road, just above the village. Return to the start (4h40).

Buttermere and Borrowdale

The Borrowdale volcanic group makes up much of the central Lake District, with crags that glower into the valleys, hem the mountain coves and confine steep gills. More than just the recent preserve of the scrambler and climber, the local rocks have been long understood for their mineral content. Mining of minerals and stone began in earnest from the 16th century across the Lakes. In this area, slate was quarried on Honister, haematite was mined in Ennerdale and graphite in Borrowdale.

Current operations are usually limited to quarrying for stone, but the legacy of mining is pervasive, and adds another dimension to the history and diversity of a popular area.

There are three routes in this section that begin in Borrowdale: a long circuit involving Great End; an easier round over Green Gable; and a short climb to Sergeant's Crag. Over Honister Pass, Buttermere and Crummock Water give another four walks: a long trek over Robinson that begins from the Newlands Valley; an intrepid journey to Pillar and Hay Stacks; a more unusual climb on High Stile; and a steep ascent to Grasmoor. Finally, there is a tour of the rounded hills around Loweswater.

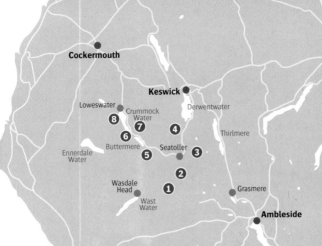

Cockermouth

Keswick

Loweswater

Derwentwater

Crummock
Water

Ennerdale
Water

Buttermere

Seatoller

Thirlmere

Wasdale
Head

West
Water

Grasmere

Ambleside

1 **Great End to Glaramara** 62
Stunning landscape on this ascent of
Great End via the celebrated Corridor
Route. Navigation skills are essential

2 **Green Gable by the Hanging Stone** 64
Tour above scenic Borrowdale to take
on Brandreth and Green Gable, with
steep ground and a waterside ascent

3 **The Eagle and the Heron** 66
Climb above Borrowdale with an easy
scramble, mild exposure and a return
by glacial moraines

4 **Robinson and Hindscarth** 68
Tackle the peaks of Hindscarth,
Robinson and Knott Rigg at the head
of the Newlands Valley

5 **Pillar and Hay Stacks** 70
Long expedition to the formidable
Pillar and charismatic Hay Stacks.
Sharp navigation is a must

6 **Traverse on High Stile** 72
Direct ascent of High Stile with brief
scrambling and exposure, descending
to the Lake District's highest waterfall

7 **Grasmoor by Hopegill Head** 74
Steep climb over two peaks, with an
easy scramble above Grasmoor's
dramatic northern combe

8 **Loweswater Highs** 76
Intricate walk that starts in woodland
to climb several small fells with a
choice of Hen Comb or Mellbreak

Great End to Glaramara

Great End (910m), Glaramara (783m)

Walk time 6h Height gain 1000m
Distance 13km
OS Map Explorer OL4 and OL6

**A varied route approached from
Borrowdale, with an exciting but
avoidable scramble by a waterfall to
start. This circuit involves steep sections
both in ascent and descent, some
awkward moves and potentially
challenging navigation.**

Start at the end of the public road at
Seathwaite in Borrowdale (GR235122). Walk
southwards through the farmyard. Directly
opposite the last in a row of farm cottages,
there is a gate to an archway on the left.

Pass through this, and take the track west.
Cross the bridge over Grains Gill, and
immediately pass through a gate on the
left. Follow the river upstream on a rough
path that soon begins to climb towards
Taylorgill Force. A short section of
scrambling provides some entertainment,
giving dramatic views of the waterfall.
When you are level with the top of the falls,
watch for a faint path that traverses the
slopes to reach a wall and Styhead Gill.
Follow the water upstream to reach a
bridge. [Variant: approach via Stockley
Bridge to avoid the scrambling.] Continue
on an improved path, past Styhead Tarn to
reach the col beyond. Bear east for about
250m and watch for a cairn-marked path to

◀ Great End from the Great Napes

the south, which starts by a short descent: this is the wonderful Corridor Route. Follow the path as it begins to climb beneath the towering crags of Great End to encounter a vast combe. Contour around the amphitheatre: initially this involves some easy scrambling, mostly in descent. The difficulties soon ease but the sense of awe remains, at least until you reach Greta Gill, whose unassuming waters have carved deep into the bedrock. Bear southeast to follow the gill upstream, leaving the main path to climb steeply under the crags of Round How to a large boggy area above. Walk east over level ground and climb grassy slopes and scree to a prominent col. Head north over jagged ground, passing Long Pike to reach the summit plateau of Great End (GR226084) (3h40). Descend southeast over very rough ground, before bearing more easily east to Esk Hause. Drop northwards to the four-pointed windbreak and then begin the undulating trek to Glaramara. A good path leads over Allen Crags and past Lincomb Tarns. There's plenty of ascent and descent, and pinpointing your position in mist can be hard. Glaramara has two summits: the further one is higher and rockier

(GR246105) (5h). Descend NNW over awkward craggy ground for 300m. Watch for a cairned path and follow this northwest over featureless grassy slopes to steep ground: the path winds close to Hind Gill but only gives rare glimpses of the wild chasm. Pass through a gate and cross the lower grassy slopes. Ford the beck and go through a gate to reach a track that leads to tea and cakes in Seathwaite (6h).

63

Green Gable by the Hanging Stone

Green Gable (801m), **Brandreth** (715m)

Walk time 4h20 Height gain 750m
Distance 11km OS Map Explorer OL4

**Fine ridge walk over two peaks, starting
from the pretty hamlet of Seatoller and
covering some rough and steep
sections once away from the paths.**

Start at Seatoller in Borrowdale
(GR245137). Walk east along the road
towards Keswick to reach a track on the
right signposted for Seathwaite
(immediately beyond Strands Bridge) after
500m. Follow this southwest towards
Thorneywaite, and take a gate on the left
just before the farm. An excellent path, the
Allderdale Ramble, leads southwest through
the dale to the farm at Seathwaite. Turn

right here, and walk about 30m through the
farmyard. Directly opposite the first in a row
of farm cottages, there is a gate to an
archway. Pass through this to take a track
west. Cross the bridge over Grains Gill and a
stile soon after to ascend by a path (with a
few slippery steps) that shadows the lively
Sourmilk Gill. After a steep climb, the
terrain levels out and leads into the wide
combe. At this point, bear south across
rough ground to the Fallen Stone, a huge
boulder calved from the steep crags of Base
Brown. Continue up to and traverse east
under the rocks, darting under the
precarious Hanging Stone and passing a
lone rowan tree. At the end of the crags,
turn to climb directly over grassy ledges to
soon reach easier ground and a narrow path.

This leads to the top of Base Brown and over the levels of Blackmoor Pols to meet the main path. Rather than follow this, traverse south into Mitchell Cove for a more interesting route to the top. Climb west over the folded ground to gain the summit plateau of Green Gable (GR214107) (2h40). Descend northeast by a wide path, then north over rocky and desolate ground to the tiny pools of Gillercomb Head. Disregarding the many chains of cairns, which only serve to confuse, climb north to the summit of Brandreth (easy to miss in bad weather). Walk NNE along the fence over the wide and occasionally boggy plateau. Where it bends to the right by a rocky notch, pass over the stile and follow another fence north to shortly cross this by another stile. Descend northwards towards Honister Hause on a

path that takes you over steep rocky ground for about 300m. Where the ground levels out, leave the path to walk east over the gentle grassy slopes of Seatoller Fell with its fine views of the imposing Gillercombe Buttress. Continue over a lumpy knoll to the fell wall. Drop north beside the wall and cross Hause Gill to reach the road where, directly opposite, a bridleway leads you at a consistent height above Borrowdale Valley. At a junction after about 800m, pass through a gate on the right to pass a stand of old pine. A track leads directly down to Seatoller (4h20).

◄ Base Brown from Seatoller Fell

The Eagle and the Heron

Sergeant's Crag (571m)

Walk time **3h40** Height gain **500m**
Distance **8km** OS Map **Explorer OL4**

A steep and sometimes exposed trek to tackle one peak, with a riverside return. Brace yourself for the steep climb with a dip in one of several enticing pools or waterfalls along the way.

Start at Stonethwaite (GR262138). (Very limited parking: drivers should consider starting from Rosthwaite or Seatoller.) Walk southeast through the village, and take the signposted footpath on the left immediately after the Langstrath Country Inn. Cross two fields and amble through the rustic campsite beside Stonethwaite Beck. Climb over a high stile in the trees, and continue past deep pools and little cascades to reach the confluence with Langstrath Beck. Follow this beck upstream, and join a track which leads to a footbridge. Cross here and continue upstream for a further 250m on the opposite bank, passing an old wall to arrive below a line of crags that runs up the fellside. Leave the path and climb steeply through the bracken towards Bleak How, beside the crags and a faint watercourse. Trend slightly leftwards where the gradient eases, level with a tier of crags and holly bushes on the left, to join a wall. Follow this to a steep band of grassy cliffs,

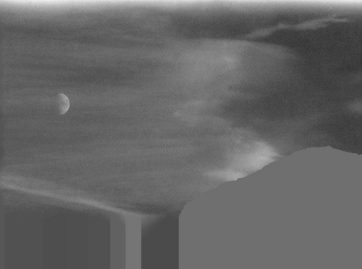

between Eagle and Heron Crags. [Escape: cross over the wall by the stile and follow a path through steep bracken down to Langstrath Beck, close to the footbridge.] Trend rightwards along a wide grassy ramp to meet a narrow gully. Climb through this, then walk rightwards along an exposed rocky terrace with a quartz banister. Now negotiate or scramble over grassy blocks in a continually entertaining climb to easy ground. Walk south along the ridge to arrive at the rocky top of Sergeant's Crag (GR273114) (2h20). Cross the fence by the fixed gate on the south side of the peak, before descending eastwards into a weird landscape of interlocking grassy moraines. Ford the head of Greenup Gill to reach a good path. Follow this northwards above the gill and all of the way down to Stonethwaite Bridge, close to the start (3h40).

Wad and whisky

According to the local tale, shepherds discovered graphite in Borrowdale in about 1500 after a violent storm uprooted trees and exposed what they thought at first to be coal. As it would not burn, the shepherds found a use for it marking sheep, but 'wad', as it was known, soon became a valuable commodity as it could be used in moulds for cannonballs and coins as well as in medicines. At one time, the 'black lead' was so valuable that a smuggling economy sprung up and armed guards had to be employed at the mines. The secret network of hidden huts and caves was later adopted by cross-border whisky smugglers and illicit distillers in the 1820s and '30s.

◀ Eagle Crag from Rosthwaite

Robinson and Hindscarth

Hindscarth (727m), **Robinson** (737m),
Knott Rigg (556m)

Walk time **5h40** Height gain **1000m**
Distance **15km** OS Map **Explorer OL4**

**A varied route that gains considerable
height over several peaks and follows
good paths, with a steep descent close
to Moss Force and a final climb with
extensive views.**

Start at Chapel Bridge by Little Town in
the Newlands Valley (GR232194). (Limited
parking: consider alternative start at
Newlands Hause.) Cross to the west side of
the bridge and immediately go through the
gate on the left to follow the private road

past the chapel and former school, gaining
gradual height to reach Low High Snab by a
gate. After passing the house, go through
another gate to join a grassy track above
Scope Beck. Higher up the valley, the track
fades to a path and winds more steeply
through quartz-streaked boulders
overlooking a small reservoir. Keep close to
the beck to reach the much flatter ground
of Little Dale. From here, cross the water,
which congregates in small pools, and
climb east over easy-angled slopes to gain
the north ridge of Hindscarth and a wide
path. Follow this until it steepens suddenly,
then for better views make a rising traverse
southeast above several steep notches to

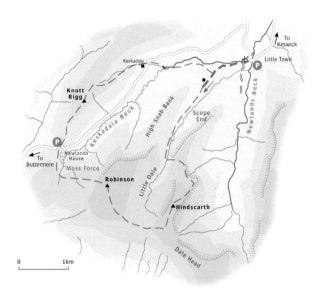

gain a subsidiary ridge above Squat Knotts.
This takes you southwards to the summit
of Hindscarth (GR215165) (2h20). Descend
south and west to Littledale Edge to begin
the gentle climb over the highest ground
to the summit of Robinson. Drop
westwards from the summit over grassy
slopes before crossing the flats of
Buttermere Moss. Rather than climb the
interlocking knolls of High Snockrigg, turn
north, making sure you keep west of the
steep ravine around Moss Beck. Join a
steep path beside the force to reach the
road at Newlands Hause (alternative start

point). Cross this and climb steeply
northeast to the top of Knott Rigg. Instead
of following the main ridge, bear east over
two bumps to descend steeply by a fine
spur. On reaching a fence around Keskadale
Farm, turn left to descend to the road. Cross
the bridge and take a marked footpath
immediately on the right. Pass through two
gates to reach a footbridge across the beck.
A good path marked with occasional posts
leads ENE, then ESE, crossing many fences
by stiles and keeping almost level to reach
the original private road to Low High Snab.
Retrace your steps to the start (5h40).

◄ Fleetwith Pike and Hindscarth from Hay Stacks

69

Pillar and Hay Stacks

Pillar (892m), **Hay Stacks** (597m)

Walk time 6h40 Height gain 1300m
Distance 13km OS Map Explorer OL4

**An extended adventure into the remote
upper Ennerdale for a steep and exposed
climb up the intimidating Pillar, and
taking in Hay Stacks on return. Good
mountain sense and route-finding ability
is a must, and scrambling skills will also
add to confidence.**

Start at Gatesgarth Farm, close to the
head of Buttermere (GR194150). Walk
through the narrow gate between
Gatesgarthdale Beck and the little postbox,
and take the fenced path to avoid the
farmyard. Cross the fields and Peggy's
Bridge, then go through a gate to climb up
beside the small plantation. Turn left, where
a good path now guides you on a steady
ascent south to the top of Scarth Gap Pass
(fine views over Buttermere). Walk over the
saddle towards Ennerdale for 350m,
watching for a cairn-marked path that heads
west from a grassy shoulder. Join this path,
which stays level above the dale, before
dropping across the slopes to reach a track.
Cross straight over this, the Memorial
Bridge and another track on the opposite
bank to begin your steep climb over cleared
and forested slopes, where a stile leads to
open country. Continue straight up by a
steep rocky gill, or take the grassy slopes
on the right side, to arrive in the wide
amphitheatre, Pillar Cove, below the main
peak and the impressive face of Pillar Rock.
Climb easy grassy slopes towards the
eastern (left) side of the crags. Now zigzag

70

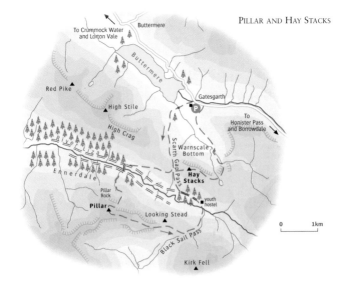

up through scree to reach the lower end of the wide rocky ramp, known as the Shamrock Traverse, that cuts across the face. Edge west along the ramp, which gives considerable exposure, before steepening up after a slippery slab. Continue diagonally rightwards across scree until the top of Pillar Rock is across a gap to the right. Then ascend steep scree to the summit of Pillar (GR172121) (3h20). Walk southeast for a short time by old fenceposts before bearing east close to the wild escarpment. A path gives easy walking, keeping to the south side of the ridge and descending steeply to Clover Stone and down to the wide col of Black Sail Pass. Descend northeast into Ennerdale and cross the bridge to the Black Sail Youth Hostel. Walk down the valley for 300m to a path on the right just before a gate and use this

to climb to the top of Scarth Gap. [Escape: retrace your steps to the start.] Rise eastwards over several craggy tiers, containing a few steep, rocky sections, to reach the summit of Hay Stacks (5h20). Despite its low altitude, the mountain boasts a diverse topography, from its heathery, tarn-pitted plateau to its giant buttresses, and a wild cragginess, much akin to Scotland's Morar. Follow rough ground eastwards to Innominate Tarn, drop past steep crags above Black Beck and continue over Green Crag towards Little Round How. Before reaching this domed crag and Dubs Quarry beyond, drop steeply north. Take a good path westwards to descend above Warnscale Beck, enjoying some of the best views of Buttermere. Cross the beck by the footbridge to continue easily to Gatesgarth Farm (6h40).

◀ Great Gable from Hay Stacks

Traverse on High Stile

High Stile (807m), **Red Pike** (755m)

Walk time **3h40** Height gain **700m**
Distance **10km** OS Map Explorer **OL4**

Challenging circuit above Buttermere, which starts by Bleaberry Tarn before climbing High Stile and Red Pike to descend by the magnificent Scale Force. Scrambling skills and a head for heights are required on this route.

Start at the Fish Hotel in Buttermere (GR175169). Walk southeast along the gravel track (public bridleway) on the south side of the hotel. Ignore a gate on the right after 300m, marked for Scale Force, and continue southwards to another gate close to the lake. Pass through the gate to follow the line of the trees, and cross the footbridge to meet a junction of several paths. Turn left and then immediately right to climb diagonally south through Burtness Woods by well-laid steps. After leaving the forest, this path doubles back to meet Sourmilk Gill and reaches Bleaberry Tarn: a great place for a snack and route-planning. Leave the tarn to climb SSE over heather and large boulders, keeping left of the bulk of Chapel Crags and close to a large dome-shaped crag at centre left. When you are almost above the dome, which now seems

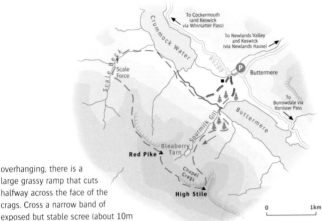

overhanging, there is a large grassy ramp that cuts halfway across the face of the crags. Cross a narrow band of exposed but stable scree (about 10m wide) to reach the ramp. Walk along this for about 100m to the highest point on the ramp where the terrain becomes more complex again. Climb the blunt arête directly over broken blocks and grass to the summit plateau of High Stile (GR167147) (2h). [Variant: walk east from Bleaberry Tarn to take the north ridge to the summit.] Follow the path WNW around the rim of the corrie before rising gently to the summit of Red Pike. Descend northwest along the fine Lingcomb Edge to reach a junction by a cairn after 1km.

Drop northwards to accompany the wide, folded ridge: a good path twists its way down through the heather, steepening as it turns west to enter the gorge of Scale Beck. Join a renovated path that zigzags down to reach a bridge below the spectacular Scale Force. Descend by one of several paths from the bridge to reach the edge of Crummock Water. Walk southeast to Scale Bridge, midway between the two lakes. Cross the bridge and follow the gravel track back to Buttermere (3h40).

The Maid of Buttermere

The daughter of a local publican, 15-year-old Mary Robinson became an unwitting celebrity in Victorian times when a travelling writer, Captain Budworth, waxed lyrical about her beauty in his best-selling *A Fortnight's Ramble in the Lakes*. Many other admirers followed but she had the misfortune of being wooed and married by one Augustus Hope, aka John Hatfield, a bigamist and fraudster who was tried for his crimes and hung in Carlisle in 1803. The original tourist attraction was remarried to a farmer from Caldbeck and died there, as Mary Harrison, in 1837.

◀ Sail Beck with High Stile and Red Pike beyond

Grasmoor by Hopegill Head

Hopegill Head (770m), **Grasmoor** (852m)

Walk time 5h Height gain 850m
Distance 13km OS Map Explorer OL4

**A route over two magnificent peaks,
with a brief scramble on an exposed spur
and some rough ground, finishing with a
short walk through woodland.**

Start at Lanthwaite at the foot of
Crummock Water (GR158207). From the
farm, walk east over the grass towards
Gasgale Gill and cross the water by the
footbridge to meet a junction of three paths.
Take the middle one to traverse through the
bracken and join the fell wall. Follow the
upper side of the wall northwards for about

2km to reach a gate at the end of an
enclosed field. After passing through the
gate, leave the path to climb beside a small
beck shaded by pine. About 200m beyond
the remains of a stone enclosure, take a
slender path on the left which makes a
rising diagonal to a craggy notch below
Dodd. Ascend the heathery central north
spur of Whiteside to reach the main ridge,
from which it is worth studying the ascent
of Grasmoor described below. An easy walk
east takes you to the summit of Hopegill
Head (GR185222) (2h20). Descend
southwards to Coledale Hause. [Escape: drop
west along Gasgale Gill to Lanthwaite.]
Rather than using any of the main paths,

cross Gasgale Gill and traverse westwards on an exciting journey that passes a small pool under broken crags to reach the savage northern combe below Dove Crags. Walk to the western rim of the combe. Although the route up looks difficult and gives an exposed position above the crags, it is mostly grassy slopes until a short rock buttress at half-height. A few moves of scrambling over stepped slabs lead to easy terrain above and the summit plateau of Grasmoor (GR174204) (3h40). Walk 200m east from the summit cairn on the plateau to descend south on a good path, which leads without difficulty along the ridge of Lad Hows

and directly down to the road above Crummock Water. Follow the path north above the road for about 600m to reach a gate on the left with a footpath marked for Scale Hill. This takes you through bracken and fine private woodland to a bench and a boathouse by the lake. Take a path on the right to climb past needle-straight pine and wind anticlockwise through the wood to reach a track and gate. Pass through the gate, crossing the field to the right of a wall to arrive at another gate and track. Follow this directly back to Lanthwaite, avoiding the farm on its north side (5h).

Loweswater Highs

Blake Fell (573m), **Hen Comb** (509m),
Mellbreak (512m), **Low Fell** (423m)

Walk time 5h20 Height gain 900m
Distance 15km OS Map Explorer OL4

**Circuit of forestry and open fell, with a
river crossing (which can be avoided by
climbing Mellbreak rather than Hen
Comb), sections of bog and an option
for refreshment along the way.**

Start by the telephone kiosk close to the
northern tip of Loweswater (GR117225).
(Good parking here.) Take the signposted
footpath southwest, passing through three
small fields to reach a farm track. Turn left
and follow the track to Hudson Place. Pass
in front of the farm buildings and go
through the gate on the left that leads to
Holme Wood. Walk along a muddy track in
the wood to a junction after 300m, marked
by three giant pine. Turn right and climb
gradually, passing the rushing Holme Force
to reach a narrow path that crosses the
track. Turn right and climb steeply through
the trees to exit the forest by a gate and
reach a stony track. Descend right here for
60m, then turn left onto a vague grassy path
above Holme Beck. Pass through a gate and
climb steeply southeast, following a narrow
watercourse to gain the quaggy plateau,
close to Carling Knott. Head southwest
along a narrow path, passing cairns and a
faint escarpment before reaching a fence.
Follow this southwards, passing under Blake
Fell: a stile just southeast of the summit
allows access to the top (GR110197) (1h40).

Keeping on the east side of the fence, descend southwards into the mire by Fothergill Head and up to the top of Gavel Fell. Cross a stile, still sticking to the east side of the ridge, and descend south over boggy terrain. Step over an old fence, and walk southeast to find a path below Floutern Cop. Follow the path for a short way to cross the next fence before climbing steeply north to reach the summit of Hen Comb. Descend north along an elegant grassy ridge until you reach a wall before a plantation. Pass over the old fence on your right, descend to Mosedale Beck and cross the river at the ford to reach a track. [Variant from Floutern Cop: continue further east along the path but, before dropping towards Scale Force, head north and climb to the summit of Mellbreak. Descend northwest to the lowest point on the plateau, and watch for a narrow path on the left. Follow this steeply down into Mosedale to join a track.] Walk north along the track past Kirkgate Farm to reach the road and refreshment at the Kirkstile Inn. After passing St Bartholemew's, turn left past the village hall and right after 150m to take the road for Thackthwaite. Turn left just before Foulsyke to enter fields by a gate. Follow the signposted path into woodland, then out of the trees by a stile, and cross a small beck at an old ruin. At this point, leave the level ground and climb steeply west. Cross a stile and continue your ascent over bracken slopes to reach scree above. A vague trail scratches leftwards to reach the fence at a gap, close to the summit of Low Fell (the higher top is a short way north). Drop down beside and cross the fence, ford Crabtree Beck and take a faint trail which contours southwest past a sheep pen and westwards around Darling Fell. Pass two cairns to gain a grassy track at an old quarry, which leads to a tarmac road at a bench. Walk up the road for 400m where a left turning takes you along a grassy track to Miresyke. Follow the road to the right, leading you back to the start (5h20).

◄ Loweswater and Mellbreak from Darling Fell

77

Wasdale, Eskdale and Dunnerdale

The drystone walls on the lower fellsides and valley floors of Wasdale, Eskdale and Dunnerdale testify to this area's hard-fought agricultural heritage. Made of local rock and capped with angled blocks to deter headstrong sheep, these walls have helped shape the landscape of the region. Against the backdrop of high and craggy mountains, the isolated whitewashed farmhouses and small settlements of the lower fells contrast with the larger but less touristic towns and villages on the western fringe.

Wasdale is the base for three routes: a steep ascent of Lingmell; a journey to Steeple with a long lakeside return; and a climb up the vast bulk of Great Gable. From Eskdale there are two routes: an entertaining round of the craggy Scafell range; and a contrasting low-level ramble from Boot. Cockley Beck is the centre for a demanding sweep of its fells, and Ulpha marks the start of a low-level but intricate walk to climb Caw. Further south, Black Combe is scaled with a pebble-strewn return along the Irish Sea.

1 Lingmell Links   80
Adventure on Lingmell with scrambling
and exposure above Piers Gill. Sharp
route-finding skills are a must

2 Steeple and The Screes   82
Big day out over Red Pike and
Haycock, with a return by the screes
of Wast Water. Stamina required

3 Hard graft on Great Gable   84
Steep route on Great Gable, arguably
the birthplace of modern rock climbing,
and Kirk Fell. Sharp navigation essential

4 Scafell Adventures   86
England's highest approached from
Eskdale over rough terrain. Keen
navigation skills and stamina needed

5 Cockley Round   88
Long but scenic circuit above the
Hardknott and Wrynose passes.
Navigation skills and stamina required

6 Eskdale Express   90
Low-level walk with plenty of
refreshment opportunities and an
easy ascent of Bleatarn Hill to finish

7 Ulpha Moonscape   92
Intricate route over the wild and
undulating Dunnerdale Fells. Good
navigation skills required

8 Black Combe Beachcomber   94
Return along the coast on this long
walk to climb one fell in a less-visited
corner of the Lake District

Lingmell Links

Lingmell (800m)

Walk time **4h** Height gain **700m**
Distance **8km** OS Map **Explorer OL6**

A fine situation above a wild chasm and a climb into the impressive corrie below Scafell Pike are just two of the highlights of this adventurous route. Scrambling skills, nerve and good navigation are required.

Start by a large car park just south of Wasdale Head (GR186084). Take the marked path northeast towards Great Gable to reach the farm at Burnthwaite after 800m. Turn left just before the farmhouse to reach a gate and pass through this onto Moses' Trod. Follow this east, ignoring the trails that branch away from Lingmell Beck. After 1km, the main path climbs to Sty Head: instead, continue along the beck until it separates into two tributaries after another 1km. Cross the one on the left just upstream and take a path that shadows the right-hand gill, which slowly unfurls as the narrow and wild ravine of Piers Gill. A path keeps fairly close to the precipice with some limited exposure but no difficulty until Middleboot Knotts. This feature is identifiable by ribbed and vertical crags on the gill side. The path leads away from the chasm towards a low buttress with a left-facing overhang, where a polished staircase just to the right of the buttress gives an enjoyable 10m scramble. The path

continues by exposed ledges and a few short moves to reach easier ground where Piers Gill turns a complete 90° and starts to diminish in height. A short traverse on the broken ground around the top of the gill takes you to a junction of paths in the complex northern cirque of Broad Crag and Scafell Pike. Follow a path westwards for 100m, turn right to a wall and follow this to Lingmell Col. Climb easily northwest to the summit of Lingmell (GR209082) (3h). Descend along the west ridge: at first this is wide and confusing in poor weather. It is easiest to keep north of Goat Crags, although afterwards you must bear southwest and cross the old wall before walking WSW over the gently sloping plateau. The ridge

suddenly becomes much more defined. A rough section over broken scree soon leads to pleasant ground and down the fell wall. Cross the stile and continue for about 300m to meet a wide path from the north. Follow this towards Wasdale Head to reach a footbridge under an old ash tree. Cross Lingmell Beck and a field beyond to return to the start (4h).

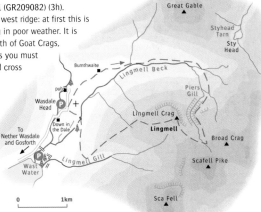

The Abraham brothers

Photography is somewhat easier today than in the time of Victorian pioneers George (1870-1965) and Ashley Abraham (1876-1951). Their equipment was heavy and awkward, yet they managed to capture images of early Lakeland climbing which had never been seen before. Many of the famous 'Keswick Brothers' images adorn the walls of the Wasdale Head Inn, which has provided refreshment to climbers for generations and considers itself the birthplace of rock climbing.

◀ Lingmell from Styhead Gill

Steeple and The Screes

Red Pike (826m), **Steeple** (819m),
Haycock (797m)

Walk time 8h Height gain 850m
Distance 22km
OS Maps Explorer OL6 and OL4

**A long but entertaining circuit of many
peaks with a descent along a rushing
beck and a return by vast screefields.**

Start at the National Trust campsite and
parking area at the head of Wast Water
(GR182074). Cross the bridge to the road
and turn left to walk southwest along the
lake. On reaching Overbeck Bridge after
1km, leave the road to follow a path on the
east bank of the beck. Pass through two
gates and climb up the riverbank to join a
wall running straight up to the imposing
spur of Yewbarrow. A path on the south side
of the wall accompanies it on a steep
journey to meet a stile before a small crag.
Cross the stile and take a path that rises
gradually, curving north under towering
buttresses. When the ground levels out,
cross the bog and the beck towards the
rocky knoll of Gosforth Crag. Climb grassy
terraces, passing the knoll on its left side by
a wide gully. Continue northwest, worming
your way through small outcrops to reach
the summit plateau, where several bumps
compete for the true top of Red Pike
(GR165106) (3h). The traverse above the
east-facing escarpment gives an
entertaining walk. Descend northwestwards
over awkward terrain and climb to the top
of Scoat Fell, bisected by an impressive
wall. Follow the wall for about 250m to a
stone circle just on its north side. [Detour: a

◂ Wasdale and the slopes of
Yewbarrow from Sty Head

cairn-marked path drops north to
Steeple, a worthwhile excursion
to appreciate the dramatic
northern combes (add 10 min).]
Continue along the wall to the
top of Haycock. Drop down the
south ridge – this steepens
slightly but gives no difficulty –
to reach boggy ground. After
walking over Pots of Ashness,
choose a convenient point to
traverse south under Seatallan
to reach the col shared with
Middle Fell. Descend south to
the marshy Greendale Tarn
and pick up a path at its foot.
Follow the path by the
rushing waters of Greendale
Gill to reach the road
(GR145056) (5h20). Turn right
past Greendale and watch for
the bridleway on the left just after
the bridge. Take the track through the trees,
turning right where it divides at the end of
woodland. Pass through a gate and walk
southwest along the track and through a
second gate. Ignore a footpath marked 'To
the lake' and continue beyond the heathery
knolls of Ashness How. After a third gate,
take a footpath marked for Woodhow
southeast towards the trees. To avoid the
farm buildings, pass through a small gate in
the wood to meet a road. Cross this, and
descend through the field opposite to reach
the river. Walk upstream, cross by a bridge
and continue on the other bank to arrive at

a building at the foot of Wast Water. Work
your way along the scree path by the shore:
the first part is the hardest over large and
stable boulders and it is worth following the
cairns for the easiest journey. Thereafter,
short runnels of scree interchange with
grassy strips all of the way along Wast
Water. From this perspective the lake
appears much friendlier than from the
western shore. Pass through several gates
at the head of the lake and over two
footbridges to reach Wasdale Head Hall.
Join the farm track, which leads back to
your start point (8h).

83

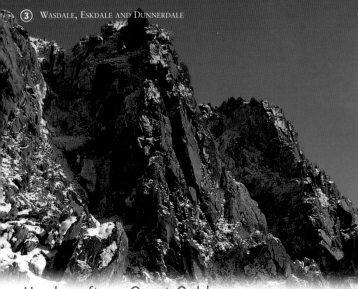

Hard graft on Great Gable

Kirk Fell (802m), **Great Gable** (899m)

Walk time **6h** Height gain **1100m**
Distance **13km**
OS Maps **Explorer OL6 and OL4**

**An ascent of two craggy giants at the
head of Wasdale, with steep climbing
and some brief exposure in descent.
Good navigation skills are a must.**

Start at the Wasdale Head Inn
(GR187087). Walk behind the pub and take
the path along Mosedale Beck, passing
through the gate and ignoring the bridge to
reach a fork after 300m. Take the left
branch along the bridleway with
increasingly dramatic views of upper
Mosedale. After a while the path begins to

climb, crosses Gatherstone Beck and
continues in switchbacks to finally reach
the top of Black Sail Pass above Ennerdale.
Cross the fenceposts and descend southeast
on a faint path for about 100m, then
contour under the buttresses and screes of
Kirkfell Crags to reach Sail Beck. Climb
steeply beside the ravine, its edges divided
into an armada of jutting prows, to reach
the gentle bowl of Baysoar Slack. Continue
easily to the summit of Kirk Fell
(GR195104) (2h40). Follow the fenceposts
eastwards over the second summit until the
terrain suddenly changes, leading to the
fractured spur of Rib End. There is a wide
and rocky path close to the apex, but false
trails may trick you north towards steep

◄ The Great Napes, with Napes Needle at bottom right

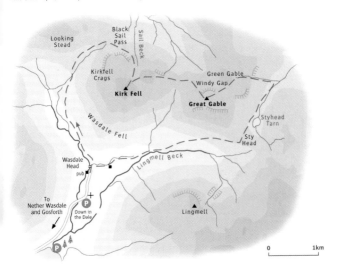

gullies so vigilance is required. Beck Head is a good point to take a breather and contemplate the next giant. [Escape: descend southwards along Gable Beck.] Gain the northwest ridge, and take a meandering scree path: higher up, chunky boulders assume prominence and give an entertaining clamber to the summit of Great Gable (GR211103) (3h40). Walk northeastwards over the plateau, where a line of cairns guides you to a path that descends steeply to Windy Gap. Drop keenly on the east side of the spur to reach a small knoll, overlooking Gable Crag to the west. A short traverse, again on the east side, leads to another steep section with a couple of awkward stretches to reach the safety of Windy Gap. Climb the short way to the top of Green Gable, shadow the cairns northeast for about 300m and then drop sharply east into Mitchell Cove. The angle soon lessens and gives very pleasant walking on soft grass. Keep to the south side of Mitchell Gill for the easiest journey down to Styhead Gill. Walk southwards to Sty Head and take the main path well below Kern Knotts and the Great Napes to join Moses' Trod. Follow this easily back to the pub where you can pretend you've walked from Skiddaw (6h).

Scafell Adventures

Esk Pike (885m), **Scafell Pike** (978m),
Sca Fell (964m)

Walk time 7h20 Height gain 1100m
Distance 19km OS Map Explorer OL6

Serious route which approaches Scafell Pike from its quieter, more atmospheric side, with an optional detour for climbers. Sharp navigation skills are a must.

Start by the telephone box at the foot of Hardknott Pass in Eskdale (GR212012). Take the track north to Brotherilkeld Farm, bypassing the farm on the left and following a path on the east bank of the River Esk through fields and into open country. Cross the humpback Lingcove Bridge beside waterfalls, and continue close to the Esk until it levels out and performs a wide loop. Leave the path here and take an ill-defined spur northwards. Level stretches

of boggy grassland alternate with steep, rocky sections to lead to Yeastyrigg Crags and the summit of Esk Pike (GR236075) (3h40). Drop northwest to Esk Hause over slabby terraces and easy slopes. Climb west under Great End along the part-renovated path to reach flatter, boulder-strewn terrain. The most direct way, which is indicated every 10m with giant cairns, keeps north of Ill Crag and south of Broad Crag. Descend with care to a col. Now follow the apex of a blocky rib to reach the summit boulderfield of Scafell Pike, England's highest mountain (GR215072) (5h). Drop SSW over jagged rocks. Competing chains of cairns radiate from the top and only serve to confuse, making it worthwhile to take a bearing in poor visibility to avoid steep cliffs. A path leads down to a spectacular position at Mickledore. [Variant for rock climbers to

◄ Bridge over Lingcove Beck in Eskdale

climb Sca Fell (rope recommended): from Mickledore, follow the spur to the cliffs of Broad Stand. Descend about 20m on the Eskdale side to a foot-wide gap between the cliff and a large boulder. Shuffle through the so-called Fat Man's Agony, teeter leftwards across a shelf and use good holds to reach a rightward trending ramp under a steep wall. Leave the ramp by climbing from the left side (exposed) or the corner (technical). Easier scrambling terrain above Mickledore Chimney leads to the summit of Sca Fell. A path takes you southwards over Slight Side (short scramble) and easily down to Eskdale (add 20 min).] For a different descent from Mickledore, drop south for 100m in distance from the mountain rescue box, hugging the east (Scafell Pike) side of the couloir. Pass under one low crag to reach a higher crag with a ruin at its foot. Walk alongside this crag on a grassy terrace (50m distance), and then descend gradually east over easy ground by a watercourse. Where this drops suddenly, traverse at the same height for a further 500m to meet the true south ridge of Scafell Pike. Enjoy fine views of the Upper Esk in the descent of this blunt rib of grass and rocks to reach a path along the valley. This leads past a magnificent waterfall and threads through giant boulders to old walls

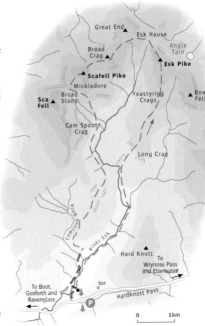

by the bend in the river. The main path rises gently here: follow it across a crag-bound basin. Beyond this, keep to the west side of the bog and wind down to join a track at Scale Bridge. Cross the bridge to reach two stiles and paths at a confusion of walls. Take either path to the farm of Taw House. Enter the farmyard, exiting by a stile on the south side to cross a field and a footbridge over the Esk. This brings you back to Brotherilkeld Farm, close to the start (7h20).

Cockley Round

Harter Fell (653m), **Hard Knott** (549m),
Swirl How (802m)

Walk time 7h40 Height gain 1100m
Distance 20km OS Map Explorer OL6

**An unusual combination of peaks on this
long but escapable route around the
source of the River Duddon, with plenty
of variety and some inspiring views of
the Scafell Group.**

Start at the picnic spot and car park by
Birks Bridge, 3km south of Cockley
Beck (GR235995). Cross the bridge and follow
the track as it bends left and rises
southwest through harvested plantation.
Pass the junction for Birks and, after 40m,
take the path on the left that leads west,
steepening as it passes through twisted

roots. To avoid an awkward climb, it is best
to follow a grassy track rightwards for
200m, make your ascent and then double
back left above the steeper ground to rejoin
the path. Pass through a gate below a small
cat-eared crag, and climb to the summit of
Harter Fell, with its many low tors. Descend
northeast with care to start and then over
easy slopes. Keep to the east side of
Demming Crag and drop to a boggy area
below. Cross a fence by a choice of stiles,
keeping to the highest ground, and recross
the fence near a small pool. Join a path to
reach the road just below the top of
Hardknott Pass. [Escape: descend east
towards Cockley Beck and follow the River
Duddon south.] Climb northwest under the
steep buttresses of Raven Crag to the top of

◀ Sca Fell from Hard Knott

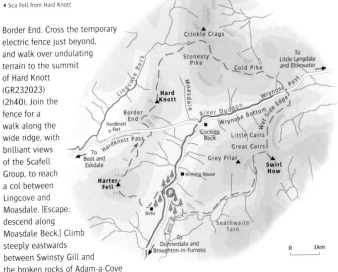

Border End. Cross the temporary electric fence just beyond, and walk over undulating terrain to the summit of Hard Knott (GR232023) (2h40). Join the fence for a walk along the wide ridge, with brilliant views of the Scafell Group, to reach a col between Lingcove and Moasdale. [Escape: descend along Moasdale Beck.] Climb steeply eastwards between Swinsty Gill and the broken rocks of Adam-a-Cove to gain easier ground. Cross the fence by the stile on the top of the ridge, and drop southeast towards Cold Pike. Rather than climb this, traverse under the southwest face using a series of natural terraces (the Gaitkins) that extend for about 1km, and keep the height above Wrynose Breast. Drop eastwards over easy slopes and cross a series of splayed grassy ribs to reach the road at the top of Wrynose Pass. [Escape: descend west along Wrynose Bottom.] Climb southwards by a steep path to join Wet Side Edge. Follow this with interest above the depths of Greenburn. Continue over the rocky top of Great Carrs and

around to the summit of Swirl How (GR272006) (6h20). Descend west into the wild combe of Calf Cove, and follow the white water of Tarn Head Beck without difficulty. Once on level ground, take the path beside Seathwaite Tarn to the dam. Continue westwards for about 1km before making a sharp turn north through crags to reach a high wall. Cross this and take the path towards the forest. Descend awkwardly through heather to the beck, and cross the fence by a stile. Turn left onto a path, which climbs through the trees on a carpet of pine needles. Easy tracks take you down to the road near the start (7h40).

Eskdale Express

Bleatarn Hill (320m)

Walk time **3h20** Height gain **200m**
Distance **10km** OS Map Explorer **OL6**

An intricate route over lowland tracks and paths to climb one hill via a folded ridge and a hidden tarn. Keen route-finding skills are a must.

Start at Dalegarth Station at the end of the Ravenglass and Eskdale Railway (GR173007). Walk northeast to the junction at Brook House Inn, and turn right (south) along a track to reach St Catherine's Church. Go around the church and cross the River Esk by smooth stepping stones, before making your way diagonally over the field beyond to a stony track. Turn right to follow the track through a gate and over Lucy Norris' footbridge, beneath a dense canopy of trees. Cross another field, with an estate wall and forest to your right, to reach an intersection of tracks. [Detour: turn left for Stanley Force.] Continue straight on to follow the Eskdale Trail through the woods and along the river to Milkingstead Bridge. Cross this and the field beyond to meet the road again. Turn left and walk west to the pub. Turn right here towards Eskdale Green

and, after 300m, take a track on the right before the railway line: this leads over the bridge towards a line of cottages. Leave the track by a path on the left before the dwellings: two kissing gates take you into open country. Climb northeast by the grassy path under small outcrops to an old ruin, and then wind eastwards, before making a prudent detour around the impenetrable bog of Siney Tarn. Continue down to firmer ground and Blea Tarn, a good picnic spot.

Walk anti-clockwise around the water and climb east through a rocky ravine. From the high point of the path, the cairned top of Bleatarn Hill is only a short detour (GR168014) (3h). Descend northeast along the path to reach a bridleway by a series of old ruins. Wander through the ruins to find a good track that descends south, taking you into the hamlet of Boot (with more refreshments). The train station is only a short walk away (3h20).

La'al Ratty

One of the most beautiful and entertaining train journeys in England is the forty-minute ride from Ravenglass to Eskdale and Dalegarth Station. Known locally as 'La'al Ratty', the line was originally founded in 1875 to transport iron ore to the coastal port but had a troubled history, facing complete closure several times over the years before being rescued by rail enthusiasts at auction in the 1960s. The various locomotives today carry up to 120,000 tourists every year between mid-March and the end of October.

◄ Eskdale from Hardknott Pass

Ulpha Moonscape

Stickle Pike (375m), **Caw** (529m)

Walk time 5h20 Height gain 700m
Distance 15km OS Map Explorer OL6

Sharpen your navigation skills for this long but relatively low-level route which starts out by the highest ground and returns by good paths above the fell wall. This walk involves lots of ascent but rewards with excellent views.

Start at a bridleway marked for Kiln Bank, about 300m south of the bridge in Ulpha, Dunnerdale (GR196930). (Parking south along the road.) Climb easily along the track to Low Birks and, just after the house, take a grassy path on the right to rise

eastwards. Where it levels out close to Hollow Moss Beck, leave the path and trend southeast to the head of the beck, maintaining height above boggy ground. Here, turn your attention to the stern southwest face of Stickle Pike: although steep, it gives an entertaining and rocky ascent to the top without any difficulties. Descend northwards, passing close to Stickle Tarn, and make your way to the top of the road at Kiln Bank Cross. Now work your way northeast, either on the lowest ground or straight over the humps: the terrain is very folded and holds many surprises. For a pleasant alternative to the wide track of Park Head Road, ascend rough

slopes to the many tops of Brown How. Drop down into the smooth bowl of Long Mire and weave your way through low crags to the summit of Caw (GR230944) (2h40). Descend eastwards, keeping to the north side of the bog and under the scraggy Pikes to reach a wall. This escorts you east to a good path above the River Lickle, which leads downstream to a gate at Stephenson Ground. Turn right between the guiding walls to follow the bridleway marked for Seathwaite, but leave this after 300m to cross Long Mire Beck on a fainter path. Keeping to the fell wall, pass Jackson Ground and ford Black Moss Beck, then climb up to a col where you can enjoy the

splendid view of Stickle Pike before swaggering down the dry watercourse. Go through a gate to reach ruins and across a field to meet the road. A right turn brings you to Hoses Farm, where you should pass through the gate on the road just beyond. Take the path on the left, which rises steeply and then accompanies the fell wall south for some distance. Pass through a gate to a grassy track, and turn right to bear west over a mish-mash of fields to a second track. This leads through two gates, bypasses Hovel Knott and climbs to a low col under Great Stickle. A choice of paths lead from here down to the road, a short walk from Ulpha (5h20).

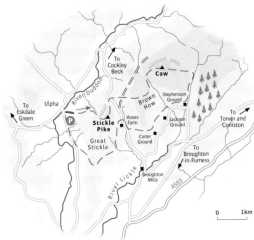

◂ Stickle Pike and Hoses Farm

Black Combe Beachcomber

Black Combe (600m)

Walk time 6h20 Height gain 600m
Distance 20km OS Map Landranger 96

A long circuit with moderate ascent that returns along a pleasant gill, past smallholdings and beside the Irish Sea.

Start at Silecroft Station, on the Barrow-in-Furness to Carlisle railway line (GR130819). Walk northeast to the war memorial on the main road. Turn left, and cross the road after 100m to take a footpath across the field and past a row of houses to the A595. Cross this road and walk along the path directly opposite to cross two fields and reach a track on the east side of Kirkbank. Follow the track above the farm for 150m to a junction and take the right fork to pass through a gate and start climbing north along a wide

grassy path. For something different, take a less-used path on the left after about 300m: this switches back and then levels out. Keep to the wide ridge, joining the main path again for a short climb until the ground levels out again. Now leave the path once more and head east to the edge of the escarpment overlooking Black Crags. The ridge takes you with interest over thick grass and heather to the summit plateau. Pass a huge cairn and continue to the top of Black Combe (GR135855) (2h20). Descend north on a path for 1km until it trends westwards along a broad spur. At this point, drop north to join a secluded beck and follow this to a confluence. Continue downstream, or alongside the fence above the east bank, to reach a track and wall. Ford the beck that runs in from the east and take the path on the right that begins with a

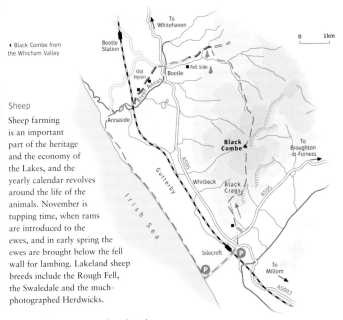

◀ Black Combe from the Whicham Valley

Sheep

Sheep farming is an important part of the heritage and the economy of the Lakes, and the yearly calendar revolves around the life of the animals. November is tupping time, when rams are introduced to the ewes, and in early spring the ewes are brought below the fell wall for lambing. Lakeland sheep breeds include the Rough Fell, the Swaledale and the much-photographed Herdwicks.

short climb to contour northwards and reach a track, just above a plantation. Descend west along the track into Bootle. Continue straight over the main road, walk west for 300m and watch for a track on the left marked for Annaside. This leads to Hyton, where you go through a gate at the farmyard entrance and pass a large barn. Cross a stile by the hedge and walk over two fields to reach Old Hyton. Pass clockwise around the shed, join the track and pass under a triple-arched bridge to accompany the river, crossing this by a footbridge. Go over the stile on the right

and walk through a narrow field. Keep the farm buildings to the left and cross two stiles to reach a track. Turn left to follow the track southwest beyond Annaside, where it merges with the Cumbria Coastal Way: this starts with a grassy track above crumbling earthen banks, and continues through fields close to the clifftop fence. Descend to the beach at Gutterby Spa (keep a look-out for dolphins). Walk 4km along the polished shingle to Silecroft Beach. Follow the road from the beach back to Silecroft and the start (6h20).

Index

Black Combe (600m)	94	**High Stile** (807m)	72
Blake Fell (573m)	76	**High Street** (828m)	36
Bleatarn Hill (320m)	90	**Hindscarth** (727m)	68
Blencathra (868m)	8	**Hopegill Head** (770m)	74
Bow Fell (902m)	54	**Ill Bell** (757m)	40
Bowscale Fell (702m)	10	**Kirk Fell** (802m)	84
Brandreth (715m)	64	**Knott** (710m)	12
Branstree (713m)	38	**Knott Rigg** (556m)	68
Calf Crag (537m)	44	**Latrigg** (368m)	14
Caw (529m)	92	**Lingmell** (800m)	80
Clough Head (726m)	26	**Lingmoor Fell** (469m)	50
Crinkle Crags (859m)	54	**Loadpot Hill** (672m)	34
Dove Crag (792m)	30	**Loughrigg Fell** (335m)	48
Eel Crag (839m)	18	**Low Fell** (423m)	76
Esk Pike (885m)	86	**Mellbreak** (512m)	76
Fairfield (873m)	46	**Pike of Blisco** (705m)	54
Glaramara (783m)	62	**Pillar** (892m)	70
Grasmoor (852m)	74	**Place Fell** (657m)	32
Great Crag (445m)	22	**Raise** (883m)	28
Great Dodd (857m)	26	**Red Pike** (Buttermere) (755m)	72
Great End (910m)	62	**Red Pike** (Mosedale) (826m)	82
Great Gable (899m)	84	**Robinson** (737m)	68
Green Gable (801m)	64	**Sca Fell** (964m)	86
Hallin Fell (388m)	32	**Scafell Pike** (978m)	86
Hard Knott (549m)	88	**Sergeant's Crag** (571m)	66
Harrison Stickle (736m)	52	**Skiddaw** (931m)	16
Hart Crag (822m)	30	**St Sunday Crag** (841m)	46
Harter Fell (653m)	88	**Steel Fell** (553m)	46
Hay Stacks (597m)	70	**Steel Knotts** (432m)	34
Haycock (797m)	82	**Steeple** (819m)	82
Helm Crag (405m)	44	**Stickle Pike** (375m)	92
Helvellyn (950m)	28	**Stybarrow Dodd** (843m)	26
Hen Comb (509m)	76	**Swirl How** (802m)	88
High Pike (658m)	12	**The Old Man of Coniston** (803m)	58
High Spy (650m)	20	**Wetherlam** (762m)	56